A COYOTE READER

A COYOTE READER

WILLIAM BRIGHT

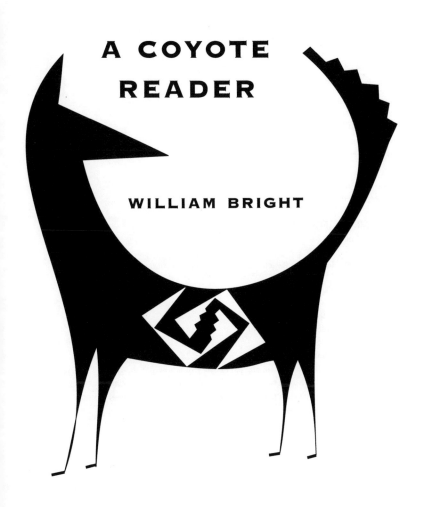

UNIVERSITY OF CALIFORNIA PRESS ▼ BERKELEY LOS ANGELES OXFORD

University of California Press
Berkeley and Los Angeles, California

University of California Press
Oxford, England

Copyright © 1993 by The Regents of the University of California

Library of Congress Cataloging-in-Publication Data

Bright, William, 1928–
    A coyote reader / William Bright.
        p.   cm.
    Includes bibliographical references and index.
    ISBN 0-520-08061-0 (cloth : alk. paper). — ISBN 0-520-08062-9 (pbk. : alk. paper)
    1. Indians of North America—Legends.   2. Indians of North America—Religion and
mythology.   3. Coyote (Legendary character).   4. Karok Indians—Legends.   5. Indian
poetry—Translations into English.   I. Title.
E98.F6B83   1993
398.24′52974442—dc20   92-32640
                                                                                   CIP

Printed in the United States of America

1   2   3   4   5   6   7   8   9

The paper used in this publication meets the minimum requirements of American
National Standard for Information Sciences—Permanence of Paper for Printed Library
Materials, ANSI Z39.48-1984 ⊗

▼▼▼
**DEDICATED TO MY GRANDDAUGHTER
ARETHA ELIZABETH BRIGHT**

CONTENTS

The traditional oral literature of Native America, specifically its mythology, is populated by personages with names like Frog, Bluejay, or Bear, and in the western part of the continent, a character called Coyote is especially important. When people with European cultural backgrounds are first exposed to Native American stories, they sometimes make false assumptions:

First, we assume that the narratives are "animal stories," and that the characters are animals of a familiar type, with a history extending from the Tortoise and the Hare, as introduced to us by Aesop, down to Mickey Mouse. It is especially tempting to think that a trickster figure like Coyote is somehow to be equated with modern tricksters like Bugs Bunny—or, for that matter, Wile E. Coyote. But in the Native American context, Frog, Bluejay, Bear, and Coyote are not animals: They are First People, members of a race of mythic prototypes who lived before humans existed. They had tremendous powers; they created the World as we know it; they instituted human life and culture—but they were also capable of being brave or cowardly, conservative or innovative, wise or stupid. They had names that we now associate with animals, and they sometimes had features, physical or psychological, that we now associate with those animals. When humans came into existence, the First People were transformed into the species of animals that still bear their names. All this is to say that the First People were not animals. They more resembled gods, although they were not much like any gods ever worshipped in Europe. If Coyote were to be compared to any divine figure of European tradition, it would be Loki of the Norsemen.

Second, our expectation of animal stories is that they have a "point," that is, sometimes they offer a moral: "The race is not to the swift." Such lessons are seldom explicit in American Indian myths, but can be inferred: When Coyote breaks a taboo by raping his daughter, she punishes him by breaking both his legs. Sometimes Old World stories offer etiological explanations: "That's why snakes crawl on the ground." This also may be true of Native American narratives on either a cosmological or a trivial level: "That's why rivers flow downstream" and "That's why bluejays have crests." When European stories lack the above elements, we expect at least some kind of resolution: "And so they lived happily ever after." In Native America, however, this is not guaranteed. In the story of the Creation, as told by the Mojave tribe of the lower Colorado River, Mastamho invents death, creates the Colorado River, ordains human institutions—and then turns into a vermin-infested fish hawk (Kroeber 1972:14). He is there still, diving for his food in the muddy water. These myths are not told to offer satisfying conclusions, they are told to account for the history of the universe.

Third, the European stereotype of animal stories is that they are primarily intended for children and occupy at best a small corner in the total literature of a people. But Native American myths are told to audiences of adults and children together, and they comprehend all the literary genres. They embrace cosmogony and religious tradition, history and law, tragedy and slapstick comedy. They contain passages of song and of dramatic dialog; their recitation, sometimes concluding with a prayer, can constitute magic, with power to stabilize the world or to gain personal advantage. They contain elements corresponding to every type of European literature: Holy Writ, entertaining or instructive tales, magical realism, or pornographic comic strip. Fourth, European tales have been codified in writing for centuries, and their full written forms are taken as more or less standard. American Indian narratives, by contrast, have been recited and transmitted orally, sometimes with relatively accurate memorization, sometimes not. Thus most stories have no single complete and "correct" form. However, since everyone hears the narratives repeatedly throughout a lifetime, the characters have become familiar archetypes, and the plots are so well known that, even in elliptical performances, the stories retain their evocative power. This creates a special problem when we attempt to convert Indian myths as told in the native languages into European languages. Many of the narratives recorded by anthropologists and linguists are difficult for English-speaking audiences to understand, not only because they lack the full cultural background, but because some elements of the narration have actually been omitted by the native storytellers. From the Indian point of view, the stories are so well known that one does not need to hear every word in order to understand their meaning. In this reader, I have tried to choose relatively full myth versions, so as to keep the need for footnotes to a minimum.

This brings us to the question of how Native American myths are best translated. Published works have adopted a variety of styles. These have included literal, word-for-word renditions for linguists; mock-biblical styles for the general reader, popular styles in the early years of the twentieth century; and bowdlerized versions for children, or for adults of delicate sensibilities. There have also been Latin renditions of the erotic passages, presumably for the use of scholars only, as when, in a Southern Paiute myth, Coyote's aunt tells him, "Affer instrumentum meum masturbationis quod ibi jacet" (Sapir 1930:338): "Bring me my dildo that's lying over there!"

Whatever other characteristics such translations have had, most of them have rendered American Indian myths as *prose*, sometimes with interpolated songs. In recent years, however, anthropological linguists like Tedlock (1972) and Hymes (1981*a*) have proposed "ethnopoetic translations," which present the texts as a form of "measured verse" and which recognize the *line* as a basic unit. The result has been a new type of translation which, when seen in print, looks a great deal like contemporary English-language poetry. Questions have been raised by many scholars as to whether the myths so translated (or indeed, Native American traditional narratives in general) are "really" poetry, or whether elements of line structure are sometimes imposed by translators. (For valuable discussions, see Bevis 1974; Huntsman 1983; Toelken and Scott 1981; and Mattina 1987.)

I have myself criticized some "ethnopoetic" practice (Bright 1982*b*), but this is not the place to discuss the details. In brief, I believe that translation of Native American texts in terms of lines has two types of value. First, it represents an effort to present the elements of phonological, grammatical, and semantic *parallelism* that exist in the originals and that are basic to their effectiveness. Second, it represents a typographic attempt to focus the attention of readers: to encourage the type of close reading that we might not accord to a page of run-on, wall-to-wall prose. In these terms, the best translator of a text is someone who knows the structure of the native language and who strives for a translation that reflects both the substance and the form of the original.

In this reader, I have given prominence to texts from the language of the Karuk (or Karok) people, spoken in the Klamath River country of Humboldt and Siskiyou counties in northwestern California. This is simply because Karuk culture and language are well known to me. As a result, these are probably the most "authentic" translations in the book. I have also included adaptations by myself, in the style of measured verse, which are based on texts transcribed and translated in prose by linguistic anthropologists from other languages: Clackamas and Kathlamet Chinook, Cupeño, Diegueño, Nez Perce, Southern Paiute, and Yana. These are languages with which I have only second-hand acquaintance, gained through interlinear texts, grammars, and dictionaries. Nevertheless, I feel that my translations have an aesthetic authenticity that is greater than that of the prose versions—and greater than any that could be produced by simply paraphrasing the prose versions without consideration of the original languages.

I became acquainted with Old Man Coyote as a myth character in 1949 during my first field work among the Karuk. I am indebted for all time to the great storytellers, no longer living, who introduced me to Coyote: Nettie Reuben, Julia Starritt, Chester Pepper, and Mamie Offield.

In 1953, in a U.S. Army installation in Nürnberg, Germany, it suddenly dawned on me that Coyote was not only a mythic figure but also my favorite literary character (though I did not yet know the term "oral literature"). I knew that I wanted, somehow, to tell the world about him. My first attempt was in a 1954 article, "The Travels of Coyote, a Karok Myth." In 1957, along with my dissertation on the Karuk language, I published in bilingual format all the Karuk Coyote stories I had transcribed.

After that, my Coyote project went on the back burner for a long time, as I occupied myself with research and teaching in India, in Washington D.C., in Berkeley, and finally for many years in Los Angeles. But in the 1970s there was a revival of interest in Native American literature, and opportunities arose for me to rethink and republish some Karuk Coyote stories— "Coyote Lays Down the Law" (1972) and "Coyote Steals Fire"

(1977)—and to edit a bilingual collection from other tribes, called *Coyote Stories* (1978).

In the same period, Dennis Tedlock and Dell Hymes, with their different but complementary viewpoints, began to develop the concepts of "ethnopoetic translation" and "measured verse" as applied to Native American traditional narratives (see Tedlock 1972; Hymes 1981*a*). I applied this approach to Karuk myths in several publications: "A Karok Myth in 'Measured Verse'" (1979), "Coyote's Journey" (1980*a*), "Coyote Gives Acorns and Salmon to Humans" (1980*b*), "Poetic Structure in Oral Narrative" (1982*a*), "A Karok Tradition: Coyote Lays Down the Law" (Bright and Reuben 1982), and "The Origin of Salmon" (Bright and Offield 1985).

Hoping that the time was at last right for me to put together a book on Coyote, I attempted to devote a sabbatical year to the project in 1980 with a fellowship from the National Endowment for the Humanities. In that year I published the following notice in *Alcheringa*, through the kindness of Dennis Tedlock, who was then editor of that journal:

A COYOTE READER

I am hoping to compile a volume with the tentative title *A Coyote Reader*, to consist of several kinds of material, both new and reprinted, written partly by myself and partly by others, about the mythic Coyote figure of the western U.S. and Meso-America. Unlike the volume of Coyote stories which I edited in 1978 for the IJAL Native American Texts Series, this book is to be entirely in English; it will be designed not only for anthropologists but also for non-specialist readers.

Some of the types of things which I hope to include are the following:

(1) Traditional Coyote stories of Native American peoples, presented in new translations which aim for greater anthropological, linguistic, and poetic validity than most of those published up to now. I think it essential that the translator KNOW THE LANGUAGE of the original (I myself am working on some translations from Karok and Cahuilla). Two particular approaches to translation seem especially valuable here:

(a) that which attempts to convey the "paralinguistic" features of natural oral performance, as Dennis Tedlock has done with Zuni texts; and

(b) that which attempts to convey the character of Native American narrative as "measured verse," as Dell Hymes has done with Northwestern materials.

(2) Commentary on the mythic Coyote figure in Native American literature, including such possible topics as these:

(a) Coyote's role in the myths of particular cultures, as in Barre Toelken's study of Navajo material.

(b) The different types of Coyote story that exist, with their respective functions, in different cultures.

(c) The relationship of the biological coyote, as studied by ethnologists like Don Gill, to the Coyote of myth.

(d) The relationship between Coyote and other trickster figures of native North America, such as Raven.

(e) The role of Coyote in Meso-American myth, both pre-Columbian and contemporary, as compared with North America.

(3) Modern literary work in English inspired by Coyote, written by poets both of Native American background (e.g., Simon Ortiz, Peter Blue Cloud) and of Anglo background (e.g., Gary Snyder, Will Staple). Add also commentary and

evaluation of such work: how and why does the mythic Coyote CONTINUE to be important to us all?

I would like anyone who is interested in this undertaking to get in touch with me: send me suggestions, references to published materials, new "ethnopoetic" translations, and unpublished MSS of poetry or commentary.

Many scholars and writers sent me materials; however, I only made limited progress during that period. In those days I used to see coyotes occasionally around my house in Los Angeles, and this somehow seemed auspicious, yet I felt that Old Man Coyote had not yet authorized me to write a book. At one point I wrote down the following lines:

When you're trying to write about tricksters
And you go downstairs at 6 A.M.
and see Coyote padding up the road,
don't think it's a good sign.
He's not there to inspire you.
Later that day, someone might steal your hubcaps.
You might not write another line that week.
Then you'll remember:
Coyote the trickster, right?
Coyote, the thief.

A few years later, receiving an invitation from Brian Swann and Arnold Krupat to contribute an essay to a book on American Indian literature, I decided that it would be a reasonable step to condense my Coyote files into article length. This I did in "The Natural History of Old Man Coyote" (1987). It seems to me significant that I was able to do the major work for that article during two peaceful periods in historic Indian cities: one in Antigua, Guatemala, the other in Oaxaca, Mexico.

It was not until 1991 that it became possible for me to take out my Coyote files again, update them, and reconstitute the book that had been originally planned. The result is this reader. It includes most of the material from my 1987 article, but brief extracts from illustrative materials are now replaced by full texts. I have also included a greater variety of materials, including new adaptations of several mythic texts. I am indebted to all the fellow scholars and coyote-poets who have given me advice and encouragement, especially Eugene Anderson, Larry Evers, Dell Hymes, José Knighton, Ken Lincoln, Lise Menn, Jarold Ramsey, Wendy Rose, Gary Snyder, Brian Swann, and Dennis Tedlock.

Finally, I thank Peter Blue Cloud, who, when I wrote him that I was interested in the mythic Coyote, sent back a postcard saying, "You sure Coyote is a myth?"

ACKNOWLEDGMENTS

Thanks go to the following for permission to reprint copyrighted material:

Robert Aitken for "Excerpts from *Coyote Rôshi Goroku*," in *Coyote's Journal*, pp. 47–48 (Berkeley: Wingbow, 1982).

Bruce Bennett for "Coyote and the Gypsies," in his *Coyote Pays a Call* (Cleveland: Bits Press, Case Western Reserve University, 1980); and for "Coyote in Love" and "Coyote's Metaphysics," *Coyote's Journal*, p. 127 (Berkeley: Wingbow, 1982).

Peter Blue Cloud for "Coyote Man and Saucy Duckfeather," pp. 29–37, and "Frybread Story," p. 65 in his *Back Then Tomorrow* (Brunswick, Me.: Blackberry Press, 1978); and for "Coyote, Coyote, Please Tell Me," in his *Elderberry Flute Song*, pp. 133–134 (Trumansburg, N.Y.: Crossing Press, 1982).

University of Chicago Press for the original version of "Coyote Baptizes the Chickens," by Alejandrina Murillo Melendres and Leanne Hinton, in *Coyote Stories*, ed. W. Bright, pp. 117–120 (Chicago, 1978). Copyright © 1978 by The University of Chicago Press.

Peter Coyote for "Muddy Prints on Mohair," in *Coyote's Journal*, pp. 43–46 (Berkeley: Wingbow, 1982).

Larry Evers for "Coyote Tricks Grey Fox," excerpt from *Ba'ts'oosee: An Apache Trickster Cycle*, a transcription and translation by Katherine Davenport and Larry Evers of a videotaped performance by Rudolph Kane, available from Clearwater Publishing Company, 1995 Broadway, New York, N.Y. 10023.

Heyday Books for excerpts from "The Creation," by William Shipley, pp. 18–19 in his *Maidu Indian Myths and Stories of Hanc'ibyjim* (Berkeley, 1991).

Dell Hymes for "Fivefold Fanfare for Coyote" (Portland, Or.: Corvine Press, 1978); for "Coyote Sucks Himself," in *In Vain I Tried to Tell You*, pp. 236–237 (Philadelphia: University of Pennsylvania Press, 1981); and for excerpts from *Spearfish Sequence*, pp. 4, 7 (Cambridge, Ma.: Corvine Press, 1981).

Lewis MacAdams for an excerpt from "Callin Home Coyote," in his *News from Niman Farm* (Bolinas: Tomboctou, 1976).

Malki Museum Press for the original version of "Coyote Cooks His Daughter," in *Mulu'wetam: The First People. Cupeño Oral History and Language*, by J. H. Hill and R. Nolasquez, pp. 60–61 (Banning, Ca., 1973); for an excerpt from "A Karok Myth in Measured Verse," by William Bright, in *Journal of California Anthropology* 1 (1979): 120–122; and for "Trickster," by Wendy Rose, in her *Lost Copper*, p. 70 (Banning, Ca., 1980).

Morrow Publishers for "Coyote and Beaver Exchange Wives," by William Brandon, in his *The Magic World*, pp. 54–56 (New York, 1971).

University of Nebraska Press for excerpts from *Reading the Fire*, by Jarold Ramsey, pp. 8–10 and 41–42 (Lincoln, 1983); and for "Coyote and the Prairie Dogs," by Yellowman, with Barre Toelken and Tacheeni Scott, in *Traditional American Indian Literatures*, ed. Karl Kroeber, pp. 65–116 (Lincoln, 1981).

New Directions Publishers for "A Berry Feast," by Gary Snyder, in his *The Back Country*, pp. 13–16, copyright © 1968 by Gary Snyder.

Ohio University Press for "Coyote and Beaver Exchange Wives," in *The Magic World*, by William Brandon (Athens, 1991). Reprinted with permission of The Ohio University Press, Athens.

University of Oklahoma Press for an excerpt from *Pueblo Animals and Myths*, by Hamilton Tyler, pp. 164–165 (Norman, 1975). Copyright © 1975 by The University of Oklahoma Press.

Simon Ortiz for "Telling about Coyote," in his *A Good Journey*, pp. 15–18 (Berkeley: Turtle Island, 1977).

Jarold Ramsey for "Coyote's Epilogue to the Telling."

Wendy Rose for "Trickster," in her *Lost Copper*, p. 70 (Banning, Ca.: Malki Museum Press, 1980).

Steve Sanfield for "Coyote Calling," in *Coyote's Journal*, p. 10 (Berkeley: Wingbow, 1982).

Leslie Silko for an excerpt from "Toe'osh: A Laguna Coyote Story," in her *Storyteller*, p. 239 (New York: Seaver, 1981).

Gary Snyder for "A Berry Feast," *Evergreen Review* 2 (1957): 119–124; reprinted in his *The Back Country*, pp. 13–16 (New York: New Directions, 1968); and for "The Incredible Survival of Coyote," in his *The Old Ways*, pp. 67–93 (San Francisco: City Lights, 1977).

Will Staple for "Coyote," in his *Passes for Human*, p. 35 (Berkeley: Shaman Drum, 1977).

Dennis Tedlock and the Trustees of Boston University for "A Coyote Reader," by William Bright, in *Alcheringa* 4, no. 2 (1980): 196.

David Wagoner for "Song for the First People," in his *Who Shall Be the Sun?* p. 14 (Bloomington: Indiana University Press, 1978).

University of Washington Press for "How Her Teeth Were Pulled," by Jarold Ramsey, in his *Love in an Earthquake*, p. 22 (Seattle, 1973).

The sheepmen complain, it is true, that the coyotes eat some
of their lambs. This is true, but do they eat enough? I mean,
enough lambs to keep the coyotes sleek, healthy and well
fed. That is my concern.
—Edward Abbey, *Desert Solitaire*

Few protagonists from the oral literature of native North Amer-
ica have achieved lasting importance in the folklore or the writ-
ten literature of Anglo-America. Of course, one thinks of Long-
fellow's *Hiawatha*, based on Algonkian narratives recorded by
Henry R. Schoolcraft and set by the poet to the meter of the
Finnish Kalevala—itself a somewhat synthetic creation; but to-
day's schoolchildren no longer memorize "By the shores of Git-
chie Gumee, / By the shining big sea water . . ." American In-
dian trickster tales are reflected somewhat indirectly in the
Bre'r Rabbit stories of Joel Chandler Harris, adapted from
nineteenth-century Black folk-narratives, which in turn prob-
ably owed a great deal to American Indian tradition of the
southeast United States; this material, too, seems to be little
read in its original form now, though it has been Disneyfied.
Competing producers of animated films and comic books may
also have drawn on the Harris stories in their creation of Bugs
Bunny—perhaps the most successful approximation to a folk-
loric trickster figure that our Anglo-American culture has yet
acquired. Yet for most of us, Bugs has no clear connection with
American Indians or, for that matter, with biology: He is really
no more a rabbit than Mickey Mouse is a mouse. A more im-
portant American Indian contribution to present and future lit-

erature may be found in Old Man Coyote—to use the name which has become familiar from many English versions of American Indian narratives.

The animal which the Aztecs called *coyotl*, a word borrowed as *coyote* by Spanish-speaking Mexicans, was first called the "prairie wolf" by Anglo-Americans who met him as they moved west across the continent; later the Mexican term coyote was borrowed, pronounced both [kayō'ti] and [ka'yōt]. Biologists gave him the Latin name *Canis latrans*. The genus name, *Canis* ("dog"), reminds us that the coyote is a member of the canid family and in fact interbreeds with the domestic dog and the wolf; *latrans* ("barking") is a rather inadequate reference to the coyote's unique howling, barking, yodeling, ululating song. During the past century, the animal has become increasingly familiar, first to inhabitants of the western United States and of Mexico but now also to people all over North America, as the coyote's range has expanded to the eastern seaboard and northward into Canada and Alaska. Coyotes have become especially familiar to many urban dwellers in cities like Los Angeles, where they have adapted to a diet that includes household garbage.

Since the days when Mark Twain published his famous description of the animal (Twain 1913:31–36), one sees the name of the coyote more and more often in print. Newspapers regularly publish accounts of the alleged menace which coyotes represent in livestock-raising areas, and of the controversies involving ranchers, conservationists, and the government over possibilities of controlling the coyote population. Along with these problems has come a great increase in biological research.[1] At the same time, Coyote has become more familiar every day in fiction, in poetry, in music—witness Joni Mitchell's hit song "Coyote"—and in the cartoons (both in film and comic-book form), which have cast Wile E. Coyote as the perennial antagonist of Beep Beep the Roadrunner.

In these latter manifestations we begin to meet not simply the biological *Canis latrans* but also a mythic figure, commonly called Old Man Coyote—the demiurge who made the world as it was known to thousands of North American Indians during the centuries before the arrival of Europeans. But Old Man Coyote, even when he brings fire for the benefit of humankind, is far from being a Promethean hero: he is an insatiable glutton, a gross lecher, an inveterate thief, liar, and outlaw, a prankster whose schemes regularly backfire. In short, Coyote is the archetypal Trickster known from literatures all over the world— Renard the Fox of medieval French legend, and Anansi the Spider of West African and modern Afro-Caribbean tradition.

Since the late nineteenth century and down to our own times, Coyote stories have been transcribed and translated by anthropologists and linguists and have also appeared in collections for the nonspecialist reader. Since the 1950s, Coyote has begun to appear more and more in the poetry and prose of Anglophone writers who have sought inspiration in American Indian tradition: Anglo writers like Gary Snyder, Native Americans like Leslie Silko and Peter Blue Cloud, and Latinos like Enrique LaMadrid. "New" Coyote stories faithful to the trickster nature of their protagonist have been produced in writing by some poets, just as American Indian narrators must have produced such narratives orally in past times. And, since the 1970s, we have seen the development of "ethnopoetics"—an effort by scholars to capture the performance values and the poetic structure of oral literature. Since this work has been carried out principally by researchers with a primary interest in Native American tradition, such as Dennis Tedlock and Dell Hymes, a natural result has been a fresh appreciation of old Coyote stories, leading to new translations that attempt to recognize and maintain the aesthetic values of the originals. It seems that Old Man Coyote can be counted among the important contributions of American Indian cultures to modern civilization, along with potatoes, tomatoes, peanuts, chocolate—and, remembering that Coyote is a trickster, we may add tobacco.

But the question is, why Coyote? There are other mythic tricksters in native North America. In the Pacific Northwest there is Raven and, sometimes, Bluejay. In the Northern Plains the trickster is sometimes called Spider; in the Southeast, he is Hare; and in most of the central and eastern continent, he has a name of his own, not identifiable with that of any animal. Yet, in the western United States—the main area of *Canis latrans* distribution at the beginning of recorded history—Coyote is the trickster par excellence for the largest number of American Indian cultures; he dominates native oral literatures of California, of Oregon, of the Plateau area inland from the northwest coast, of the Great Basin, of the Southwest, and of the Southern Plains (see Ramsey 1983:25–26). Is there, perhaps, something about the behavior of the biological coyote that makes him especially fit for the role of mythic trickster? Similarly, we may ask: Of all possible tricksters, why is it that Coyote has captured the imagination of so many English-speaking writers and audiences? One aim of this chapter, then, is to explore relationships between the behavior of the biological coyote and the character of Old Man Coyote as the most important trickster figure of native North America, and by extension to examine the continuing symbolic importance of Coyote for us human beings who share a continent with him. The nature of the data and discussion is such that we will not be able to reach anything like a scientific proof or a predictive statement. Rather, as in a traditional Native American narration, the purpose is to amuse the audience when Coyote plays the fool, to shock it when Coyote commits incest or murder, to edify it when Coyote gets his comeuppance—and beyond all that, through quotation and example more than through analysis, to expand our understanding of vhat is possible, to perceive connections previously unnoticed, .nd to see human nature more clearly as reflected in Coyote.

A NOTE ABOUT TERMINOLOGY

When appropriate, I distinguish the biological *Canis latrans*,)r simply (lowercase) coyotes, from the mythic trickster, Old Man Coyote, or simply (uppercase) Coyote. But since these two ypes tend to merge in human consciousness, the presence or ibsence of capital "C" should not be taken too seriously. Also, with apologies to all female coyotes, I should note that individ- ials of unspecified gender will be routinely referred to here as 'he" simply for ease of comparison with mythic Coyote, who is isually male (see Ramsey 1983:200 n. 1). By contrast, I refer to he species *Homo sapiens* by terms such as "human beings" or 'humankind," rather than "Man(kind)"—even though in quo- ations we are stuck with the generic masculine.

Before there was a written American literature in English, there was an oral American literature in the hundreds of Native American languages. And in dozens of the Native traditions of western North America we find Coyote, present at the very creation of the universe, as in this account from the Maidu tribe of northern California (Shipley 1991:18–19).

> And Earthmaker, they say,
> when this world was covered with water,
> floated and looked about him.
>
> As he floated and looked about,
> he did not see anywhere, indeed,
> even a tiny bit of land.
>
> . . . Thereupon, he sang.
>
> "Where are you, little bit of earth?"
> He said it, singing.
> He kept singing and singing.
>
> . . . Coyote said:
> "Indeed, there are not many songs that I don't know."
> And then, after that, *he* sang,
> kept on singing and singing.

Together, Earthmaker and Coyote discover a bird's nest, which they stretch with ropes until it becomes the Earth. Together,

hey create the inhabitants of the Earth and ordain the princi-
ples of life.

Some eons later, America is "discovered" by Europeans. As
Anglo-Americans spread across North America in the nine-
teenth century, the first written mentions of Coyote begin to ap-
pear. In one of the earliest and best known of these, by Mark
Twain, Coyote appears in a double aspect. To be sure, he is an
unprepossessing member of the animal kingdom—"a long,
slim, sick and sorry-looking skeleton, with a gray wolf-skin
stretched over it, with . . . a general slinking expression all over"
(1913:32). But Coyote is also a figure of tall tales, indeed a leg-
endary trickster whom Twain describes with unconcealed sym-
pathy (1913:31–36).

▼▼▼
THE COYOTE

From Chapter 5 of *Roughing It*, by MARK TWAIN, volume 1.]

Along about an hour after breakfast we saw the first
prairie-dog villages, the first antelope, and the first wolf. If
I remember rightly, this latter was the regular *coyote* (pro-
nounced ky-*o*-te) of the farther deserts. And if it *was*, he
was not a pretty creature, or respectable either, for I got
well acquainted with his race afterward, and can speak with
confidence. The coyote is a long, slim, sick and sorry-
looking skeleton, with a gray wolf-skin stretched over it, a
tolerably bushy tail that forever sags down with a despair-
ing expression of forsakenness and misery, a furtive and
evil eye, and a long, sharp face, with slightly lifted lip and
exposed teeth. He has a general slinking expression all
over. The coyote is a living, breathing allegory of Want. He

is *always* hungry. He is always poor, out of luck and friendless. The meanest creatures despise him, and even the fleas would desert him for a velocipede. He is so spiritless and cowardly that even while his exposed teeth are pretending a threat, the rest of his face is apologizing for it. And he is *so* homely!—so scrawny, and ribby, and coarse-haired, and pitiful. When he sees you he lifts his lip and lets a flash of his teeth out, and then turns a little out of the course he was pursuing, depresses his head a bit, and strikes a long, soft-footed trot through the sage-brush, glancing over his shoulder at you, from time to time, till he is about out of easy pistol range, and then he stops and takes a deliberate survey of you; he will trot fifty yards and stop again—another fifty and stop again; and finally the gray of his gliding body blends with the gray of the sage-brush, and he disappears. All this is when you make no demonstration against him; but if you do, he develops a livelier interest in his journey, and instantly electrifies his heels and puts such a deal of real estate between himself and your weapon, that by the time you have raised the hammer you see that you need a minie rifle, and by the time you have got him in line you need a rifled cannon, and by the time you have "drawn a bead" on him you see well enough that nothing but an unusually long-winded streak of lightning could reach him where he is now. But if you start a swift-footed dog after him, you will enjoy it ever so much—especially if it is a dog that has a good opinion of himself, and has been brought up to think he knows something about speed. The coyote will go swinging gently off on that deceitful trot of his, and every little while he will smile a fraudful smile over his shoulder that will fill that dog entirely full of encouragement and worldly ambition, and make him lay his head still lower to the ground, and stretch his neck further to the front, and pant more fiercely, and stick his tail out

straighter behind, and move his furious legs with a yet
wilder frenzy, and leave a broader and broader, and higher
and denser cloud of desert sand smoking behind, and
marking his long wake across the level plain! And all this
time the dog is only a short twenty feet behind the coyote,
and to save the soul of him he cannot understand why it is
that he cannot get perceptibly closer; and he begins to get
aggravated, and it makes him madder and madder to see
how gently the coyote glides along and never pants or
sweats or ceases to smile; and he grows still more and more
incensed to see how shamefully he has been taken in by an
entire stranger, and what an ignoble swindle that long,
calm, soft-footed trot is; and next he notices that he is get-
ting fagged, and that the coyote actually has to slacken
speed a little to keep from running away from him—and
then that town-dog is mad in earnest, and he begins to
strain and weep and swear, and paw the sand higher than
ever, and reach for the coyote with concentrated and des-
perate energy. This "spurt" finds him six feet behind the
gliding enemy, and two miles from his friends. And then, in
the instant that a wild new hope is lighting up his face, the
coyote turns and smiles blandly upon him once more, and
with a something about it which seems to say: "Well, I shall
have to tear myself away from you, bub—business is busi-
ness, and it will not do for me to be fooling along this way
all day"—and forthwith there is a rushing sound, and the
sudden splitting of a long crack through the atmosphere,
and behold that dog is solitary and alone in the midst of a
vast solitude!

It makes his head swim. He stops, and looks all around;
climbs the nearest sand-mound, and gazes into the dis-
tance; shakes his head reflectively, and then, without a
word, he turns and jogs along back to his train, and takes
up a humble position under the hindmost wagon, and feels

unspeakably mean, and looks ashamed, and hangs his tail at half-mast for a week. And for as much as a year after that, whenever there is a great hue and cry after a coyote, that dog will merely glance in that direction without emotion, and apparently observe to himself, "I believe I do not wish any of the pie."

The coyote lives chiefly in the most desolate and forbidding deserts, along with the lizard, the jackass-rabbit and the raven, and gets an uncertain and precarious living, and earns it. He seems to subsist almost wholly on the carcasses of oxen, mules, and horses that have dropped out of emigrant trains and died, and upon windfalls of carrion, and occasional legacies of offal bequeathed to him by white men who have been opulent enough to have something better to butcher than condemned army bacon. . . .

. . . He does not mind going a hundred miles to breakfast, and a hundred and fifty to dinner, because he is sure to have three or four days between meals, and he can just as well be traveling and looking at the scenery as lying around doing nothing and adding to the burdens of his parents.

We soon learned to recognize the sharp, vicious bark of the coyote as it came across the murky plain at night to disturb our dreams among the mail-sacks; and remembering his forlorn aspect and his hard fortune, made shift to wish him the blessed novelty of a long day's good luck and a limitless larder the morrow.

Subsequent years have produced an increasing amount of Coyoteana in English, including the work of folklorists, natural historians, biologists, anthropologists, linguists—and, in recent decades, a growing number of literary scholars, poets, and other creative writers.

A type of Coyote literature that has become well established in the twentieth century is that kind of popular writing which

ombines informal and anecdotal natural history observations
n *Canis latrans* with folkloristic accounts of Old Man Coyote.
Both Spanish American and Native American sources are likely
o figure in such works.[1] This class of writing overlaps to some
xtent with the coyote literature produced by biologists, espe-
ially those concerned with ecological aspects of coyote behavior
see Murie 1940; Young and Jackson 1951; Pringle 1977; and
Bekoff 1978). Such works give a revealing picture of those char-
cteristics of Coyote that have enabled him to fill so well the role
f trickster in oral and written literature. A closely related field
f study looks at the ecology of the coyote in urban areas, giving
pecial attention to his ability to adapt and survive (see Gill
970; Gill and Bonnett 1973:87–108).

A different type of attention, focusing on the transcription,
ranslation, and interpretation of American Indian traditions,
as been pursued by anthropologists and linguists since the late
ineteenth century. Monuments of this literature, presented by
uch scholars as Franz Boas, Edward Sapir, and A. L. Kroeber,
an be found in serial publications such as the *Annual Report* and
he *Bulletin* of the Bureau of American Ethnology (in the Smith-
onian Institution); in the *Publications* of the American Ethno-
ogical Society; in the *Publications in American Archaeology and
Ethnography* of the University of California; and, in more recent
ears, in the *Publications in Linguistics* of the University of Cali-
ornia and in the *Native American Texts Series* published by the
University of Chicago as a supplement to the *International Jour-
nal of American Linguistics*.[2] In all these sources, as might be ex-
pected, tricksters make frequent appearances. And, in mate-
rials from California, from the Plateau and Great Basin areas,
nd from the Southwest, the trickster role is frequently played
by Old Man Coyote. The value of these materials lies in their
uthenticity, especially for readers who are able to follow the na-
ive language texts. Their weakness is that the technical linguis-
ic format and the awkward literal translations have tended to

limit readership to an academic audience. There have also been some books intended to present English translations of Coyote stories in nontechnical format and relatively popular style; these, whatever the authenticity of their sources, lose much of the "feel" of the Native American originals. The best such work is clearly that of Jarold Ramsey, who adds the extra dimension of being a gifted scholar in English literature.[3]

A direct outgrowth of the anthropological-linguistic tradition in the presentation of Native American texts is that which can be called "ethnopoetic." The term, and the group of approaches that it covers, were introduced in the journal *Alcheringa*, inaugurated under the editorship of Jerome Rothenberg and Dennis Tedlock in 1970. The two editors subsequently took separate routes: Rothenberg, more the poet and literary scholar, developed his controversial method of "reinterpreting" American Indian literature—as previously translated by anthropologists and linguists—in terms of contemporary English-language poetry. As might be expected, Coyote as trickster appears again in these materials.[4] Tedlock, more the linguistic anthropologist, has focused rather on translations that are as faithful as possible to the originals and on a verse format that reflects the poetic qualities inherent in traditional performance.[5]

A somewhat different but also linguistically oriented approach has been that of Dell Hymes, who has reanalyzed the structure of published texts from societies in which narrative traditions are now extinct or moribund and has shown that such texts can best be appreciated not as prose but as "measured verse." Here, units such as lines and stanzas are defined not by the phonological units of old-world verse, such as rhyme, meter, or syllable count, but rather by morphosyntactic, lexical, and semantic features (see Hymes 1981a). Other scholars have experimented profitably with the approaches of both Tedlock and Hymes. And of course Old Man Coyote makes frequent appearances in all this work. In the chapters that follow, I will samɔle Coyote stories in several ethnopoetic traditions. They are by preference those that follow Hymes's model and they include my own translations from the Karuk language of California.[6]

Parallel with ethnopoetic work on Native American narrative, there has grown up what might be called, in contrast, a "neopoetic" literature in which poets and other creative writers of Anglo, Latino, and Native American background have introduced Old Man Coyote and other figures of oral tradition into their own English-language work. There seems little doubt that the entrance of Coyote into contemporary poetry was given its major impetus by Gary Snyder in his poem "A Berry Feast," originally published in the historic Grove Press collection (1957:110–114) that first drew wide attention to the "beat" poets of the San Francisco area.

Snyder here introduces Coyote as the self-contradictory trickster, an "old man," yet a puppy; "ugly" and self-indulgent, yet the "bringer of goodies." Coyote announces that "The people are coming"—the human species, the Indians for whom provision should be made: "you will grow thick and green, people / will eat you, you berries!" The end of the poem, however, depicts Coyote as outliving humanity, whether Indian or Anglo. He is the ultimate survivor.

▼▼▼

A BERRY FEAST

[By GARY SNYDER. Published in *Evergreen Review*. Reprinted in *The Back Country*.]

I

Fur the color of mud, the smooth loper   *coyote*
Crapulous old man, a drifter,
Praises! Of Coyote the Nasty, the fat

Puppy that abused himself, the ugly gambler,
Bringer of goodies.

In bearshit, find it in August   *berries*
Neat pile on the fragrant trail, in late
August, perhaps by a larch tree,
Bear has been eating the berries.
      high meadow, late summer, snow gone
Blackbear
        eating berries, married
To a woman whose breasts bleed
From nursing the half human cubs.

Somewhere of course there are people.   *people*
Collecting and junking, gibbering all day,

"Where I shoot my arrows   *coyote*
"There is the sunflower's shade
        song of the rattlesnake, coiled
        in the boulder's groin
"K'ak, k'ak, k'ak!"
        sang Coyote. Mating with
        humankind.

The Chainsaw falls for boards of pine,   *people*
Suburban bedrooms block on block
Will waver with this grain and knot,
The maddening shapes will start and fade

Each morning when Commuters wake.
Joined boards hung on frames,
        a box to catch the biped in.

        and shadow swings around the tree   *berries*
Shifting on the berrybush
        from leaf to leaf across each day
The shadow swings around the tree

II

Three, down, through windows   *people*
Dawn-leaping cats, all barred brown, gray
Whiskers aflame
    bits of mouse on the tongue

Washing the coffeepot in the river
    the baby yelling for breakfast
Her breasts, black-nippled, blue-veined,
                heavy,

Hung through the loose shirt
    squeezed, with the free hand
    white jet in three cups.
Cats at dawn
    derry derry down.

Creeks wash clean where trout hide   *coyote*
We chew the black plug
Sleep on needles through long afternoons
    "You shall be owl
    "You shall be sparrow
    "You will grow thick and green, people
    "Will eat you, you berries!"
Coyote: shot from the car, two ears,
A tail bring bounty.

Clanks of tread   *people*
    oxen of Shang
    moving the measured road
Bronze bells at the throat
Bronze balls on the horns, the bright Oxen
Chanting through sunlight and dust
    wheeling logs down hills
    into heaps,
              the yellow

Fat-snout Caterpillar, tread-toppling forward
Leaf on leaf, roots in gold volcanic dirt.

When   *berries*
snow melts back
        from the trees
bare branches   knobbed pine twigs
        hot sun on wet flowers
green shoots of huckleberry
breaking through snow.

III

Belly stretched taut in a bulge   *people*
Breasts swelling as you guzzle beer, who wants
                    Nirvana?
Here is water, wine, beer
Enough books for a week
A mess of afterbirth
A smell of hot earth, a warm mist
Steams from the crotch

"You can't be killers all your life   *coyote*
"The people are coming—"
        —and when Magpie
Revived him, limp rag of fur in the river
Drowned and drifting, fish-food in the shallows,
"Up yours!" sang Coyote
                    and ran.

Delicate blue-black, sweeter from meadows   *berries*
Small and tart in valleys, with light blue dust
Huckleberries scatter through pine woods
Crowd along gullies, climb dusty cliffs,
Spread through the air by birds;
Find them in droppings of bear.

"Stopped in the night   *people*
"Ate hot pancakes in a bright room
"Drank coffee, read the paper
"In a strange town, drove on,
            singing, as the drunkard swerved the car
"Wake from your dreams, bright ladies!
"Tighten your legs, squeeze demons from
            the queynt with rigid thighs
"Young red-eyed men will come
"With limp erections, snuffling cries
"To dry your stiffening bodies in the sun!"

Woke at the beach. Gray dawn,
Drenched with rain. One naked man
Frying his horsemeat on a stone.

IV
Coyote yaps, a knife!   *coyote*
Sunrise on yellow rocks.
People gone, death no disaster,
Clear sun in the scrubbed sky
            empty and bright
Lizards scurry from darkness
We lizards sun on yellow rocks.

See, from the foothills   *berries*
Shred of river glinting, trailing
To flatlands, the city:
            glare of haze in the valley horizon
Sun caught on glass gleams and goes.
From cool springs under cedar
On his haunches, white grin,
            long tongue panting, he watches:

Dead city in dry summer,
Where berries grow.

[NOTE: *The berry feast is a first-fruits celebration that consumes a week of mid-August on the Warm Springs Indian Reservation in Oregon. Coyote is the name for the Trickster-Hero of the mythology of that region. I pronounce "coyote" with the accent on the second syllable and the final* e *sounded.*]

Snyder, not only as poet but also as essayist, has focused on Coyote. In "The Incredible Survival of Coyote" he sums up a motif found in dozens of Indian myths: "Coyote never dies, he gets killed plenty of times, but he always comes back to life again, and then he goes right on traveling" (Snyder 1977:71). The persistence of Coyote is reflected, as Snyder illustrates, in the work of a growing number of contemporary poets.[7] It is also reflected, as biologists like Marc Bekoff and ecologists like Don Gill have shown us, in the current findings on *Canis latrans*: increasing geographic spread, improving adaptation to urban living, and ineffectiveness of efforts at predator control.

Coyote is, then, many things. Like humanity, he is an omnivorous, ubiquitous inhabitant of the North American biosphere; he is a mythic trickster, responsible for the world as we know it, yet a persistent bungler and dupe; and he is now, for many whites as well as for Indians, a powerful symbol of a viewpoint that looks beyond abstractions and beyond technology to the ultimate value of survival.

As I have noted, Native American "Coyote stories" occur over a wide geographical area, ranging at least from British Columbia to Guatemala, and from the Pacific Ocean to the Great Plains. However, the role of Coyote as a figure of narrative varies greatly over this area. It is in the Great Basin, the Plateau (eastern Washington and Oregon, Idaho, and adjacent areas) and in California where we are most likely to find Old Man Coyote as prototypical mythic trickster. As we move farther south, we find that Coyote can move from mythic into modern times; thus, the Diegueño of Baja California relate how he baptizes the chickens, and the Comanche of the southern plains tell how he tricks white soldiers and preachers (see Hinton 1978; Buller 1983). Southwestern tribes often have stories in which several coyotes appear. In Mesoamerica Coyote is still a shifty trickster but seldom a successful one, and he is never the "bringer of goodies"; he is almost invariably a bungler and dupe.

One must suppose that this picture involves several historical strands (including some from European folktales, especially in Latin America). However, the prototypical Old Man Coyote can perhaps be identified as the figure best known from the tribes of California, the Great Basin, and the Plateau region, and it is to this concept of Old Man Coyote that I will generally refer below (though I may not be able to resist quoting some especially effective Coyote stories from other areas).

A basic fact about Old Man Coyote, then, is that he was a

unique individual and was one of the First People—the race of beings who occupied the world in the mythic times before humans came into existence. Sometimes Coyote is spoken of as having a wife and children, but it is not necessarily implied that they are also coyotes; certainly Coyote is known to mate promiscuously with females such as Frog or Mouse. The First People have names that we now associate with animals, or occasionally with plants and other natural phenomena, and Indians sometimes refer to the mythic period as "the time when animals were people." However, the First People do not seem to have been unambiguously either human or nonhuman in form; since they frequently possess great magical powers, they alter their shapes at will. Among some tribes (though not the Karuk), a figure identifiable as the Creator or Old God is also identifiable as coeval with the First People but set apart from them; he may be responsible for the world in which the First People live, but he plays little part in the subsequent events that lead to the existence of human beings and of the world which we now know. For some tribes, the First People include a noble, heroic figure, such as Wolf among the Comanche (see Buller 1983) and the Chemehuevi (Laird 1984), who foresees the coming of humanity and plans a perfect, ideal world for them—until his brother Coyote enters the scene as marplot. But concurrent with the creation of man is a great change, whereby the First People are transformed into all the species of animals and plants which we know today—as well as heavenly bodies, mountains, and rocks—and, in some cases, disembodied spirits. All these bear the same names as before, and indeed cannot be differentiated from the First People; as Barre Toelken says (1971:204),

There is no possible distinction [for the Navajo] between Ma'i, the *animal* we recognize as a coyote in the fields, and Ma'i, the *personification* of Coyote power in all coyotes, and Ma'i, the *character* (trickster, creator, and buffoon) in legends and tales, and Ma'i, the symbolic character of *disorder* in the myths. Ma'i is not a composite but a complex; a Navajo would see no reason to distinguish separate aspects.

Among the First People, Coyote stands out in several respects. For one thing, stories in which he figures are especially numerous and popular. In most of these stories, he is the multifaceted North American trickster figure who was discussed at length by Paul Radin with particular reference to psychological interpretation of the Jungian school.[1] Further light has been shed on this trickster role by M. L. Ricketts (1965), writing from the viewpoint of comparative religion; by Toelken, with particular reference to Coyote as a character in Navajo narratives (see also Toelken and Scott 1981); and, most recently, for western Native America in general, by J. Ramsey (1973:24–46). It should be understood, however, that "trickster" in this context does not simply refer to some kind of practical joker, but rather to what Ricketts terms the "trickster-transformer-culture hero." The trickster steals fire and salmon for the benefit of humans, lays down cultural roles for men and women, and even ordains death, but is at the same time "a prankster who is grossly erotic, insatiably hungry, inordinately vain, deceitful, and cunning . . . and a blunderer who is often the victim of his own tricks." In most traditions he does not act as original creator; rather, "he changes things into the forms they have retained ever since"— he is the creator of "the world-as-it-is" (Ricketts 1965:327, 341). To be sure, he is no altruist; he acts out of impulse, or appetite, or for the pure joy of trickery. Yet his most obscene or amoral exploit is, for human beings, something more than material for humor. Toelken quotes his Navajo consultant, Yellowman, as saying: "If he did not do all those things, then those things would not be possible in the world." In Toelken's paraphrase, Coyote is "the exponent of all possibilities" (1976:76, 164).

One cannot read many Coyote stories without being struck

by the degree to which his creativity, his adaptability, his unreliability, and his buffoonery are reminiscent of the genus *Homo* (in this context, *sapiens* should perhaps only be added with a "[*sic!*]" after it). Ricketts goes so far as to say that "the trickster is man"—or later, with some qualification, that he is "the personification of all the traits of man raised to the highest degree"; in contrast to the type of religion which conceives of a transcendent god, the trickster "is a symbol of mankind, the race which, according to this mythic vision, is unconquerable and immortal" (1965:336, 347, 349). Similarly, Ramsey refers to the trickster as "all man's epitome," as "an imaginary hyperbolic figure of the human"—or perhaps more precisely as a Lévi-Straussian "mediator" who links the world of humanity, with all of its curiosity, self-awareness, and resultant "cultural" baggage, to the "natural" world of animals. Ramsey emphasizes Coyote's role as the bricoleur, the handyman or fixer-upper, who cannot stop himself from tampering with Original Creation and thus produces the world which we humans now know—imperfect, but *ours* (1973:25, 27, 41).

It is, then, an oversimplification to say that Coyote is really *Homo sapiens*; he is also, in many significant ways, *Canis latrans*. As Ramsey notes, some of the most prominent trickster figures, such as Coyote and Raven, are scavengers and omnivores, and thus—like humans!—can be seen as symbolizing an equivocal middle position between herbivores and carnivores (1973:29). Among many tribes, the trickster is called by some form of the epithet "Old Man"; thus, in Karuk, coyotes are called *pihnêefich*, which is etymologically "Shitty Old-Man"—probably referring to tales of the trickster's coprophagy. Elsewhere, especially in the Plains area, the trickster has names of ostensibly human type, but Coyote has many nicknames in various languages— for example, in Karuk, *tishráam ishkuuntíhan*, "He who lurks in the grassy places."[2]

In fact, I wish to propose that, in the areas where coyotes

were best known to Native Americans in pre-Columbian times, *Canis latrans* was an especially appropriate actor—biologically, ecologically, and ethnologically—to play the trickster role. From this, I suggest, has followed the widespread significance of Old Man Coyote in Native American mythic traditions. From this mythic role in turn, along with Coyote's biological characteristics—especially his striking talents as a survivor—has arisen his increasing importance as a figure in English-language literature. In the following discussion, I will attempt to show how some of the attributes of Coyote as trickster and survivor are reflected in correlations between zoological observation, Native American myth, and contemporary poetry.[3]

Myths from many tribes begin with variants on the words used as the title of Jarold Ramsey's book *Coyote Was Going There* (1977). In the myths of the Karuk, Coyote makes at least two trips up the Klamath River to "the upriver end of the world" (sometimes referred to by Indians as "the North Pole," but more likely to be identified as Klamath Falls, Oregon). In one myth he brings back fire to "the center of the world"—the confluence of the Salmon and Klamath rivers, at Somes Bar, California (Bright 1979). In the cycle which I have called "Coyote's Journey" (Bright 1980*b*), he travels far north to seek money, but falls into the river and winds up at "the downriver end of the world," that is, the ocean; eventually he returns to his home in Karuk country. No other mythic character so traverses the entire length of the Karuk universe.

The following portion of the cycle describes part of Coyote's downriver odyssey (Bright 1980*b*:39–41).

▼▼▼

COYOTE GOES TO A DANCE

[Told in Karuk by MAMIE OFFIELD. Translated with WILLIAM BRIGHT.]

And then he traveled on,
   Coyote did,

    he turned back into a person,
        he turned back into himself.
And then he saw,
    there they were having a puberty dance.
So he joined the "flower dancing,"
    he carried the girl around,
        the menstruant girl.
And then she became pregnant.
And then Coyote ran away.
And then they chased him,
    they said,
        "He's the one that did that mischief."
And then he ran,
    they were about to catch him.
And then he peeled back his foreskin in a hollow tree,
    he said,
        "You people come out, come out!"
And then ants came out,
    winged ants,
        that's why they call them that,
            "Coyote-peeling-back-his-foreskin."
And they stopped,
    the ones who were chasing him,
        they looked,
            they said, "What's that?"
And by this time Coyote was far away.
And then they were about to catch him again.
And then he urinated in a hollow tree.
And then some came out,
    they flew out,
        those birds,
And then the ones chasing him stopped,
    they looked,
        they said, "What's that?"—

that's why they're called "little-Coyote-urine,"
   wild canaries.
And then he ran downstream to a place uphill from Requa.
And there was a big mountain sitting there.
And then he said,
   "Get little, get little!"
And then he ran down the other side.
And then he crawled indoors,
   into a sweathouse,
And then they ran down from upstream,
   the ones chasing him.
And then they looked inside,
   into the sweathouse.
And then they said,
   "Did you see him anywhere,
     a person?"
And then Coyote said,
   "Me no savvy."[1]
And then they said,
   "I think he's saying,
     Coyote's already downstream."
And then Coyote jumped out.
And then he ran downhill,
   he jumped into a boat,
     and he paddled acrossriver.
And then he said,
   "Mice, come here!
"Gnaw holes in them,
   those boats."
And then they gnawed holes in them,
   the boats.
And then they said,
   the ones chasing him said,
     "I bet that was him,

    the one sitting in the sweathouse."
And then they ran back the other way,
    there he was on the opposite shore.
And then they launched the boats,
    but they sank,
        because the mice had gnawed them.

The concluding portion of the cycle describes Coyote's return
from the seacoast to his home on the central course of the Klam-
ath River (Bright 1980*b*:41–45).

▼▼▼
COYOTE'S HOMECOMING

[Told in Karuk by CHESTER PEPPER. Translated with WILLIAM
BRIGHT.]

Coyote wandered around there,
    there was a sweathouse standing.
And he looked inside,
    he saw nobody at all.
And Coyote crawled in.

And when he got inside,
      when he looked around,
        all the chairs were made of pure grease,
          their headrests too were of grease,
            and their stepladder too was of grease.
And Coyote was hungry.
And he thought,
    "I'll just taste them,
      those headrests."
And when he took a taste,
    they were very delicious.

Finally he ate them all up,
    he ate up their stepladder too.
Then suddenly he sort of heard something.
And he thought,
    "I'd better hide."
And he lay down there behind the woodpile.
And when the men came back in the sweathouse in the
                                      evening,
        as each man crawled in,
        he fell down.[2]
And they said,
    "I'm thinking,
        Coyote's wandering around here.
"That's who did it,
    he ate them all up,
        our headrests."
He just lay there,
    he heard them,
        when they were talking about him.
And then they said,
    "Let's spend the night away from home,
        at Long Pond."
And then he thought,
    Coyote thought,
        "They're talking about my country."
And he jumped out—
    "Nephew, my nephews,
        I'll go along!"
And they said, "All right,
    but don't open your eyes."
"All right, I'll do that,
    I won't open my eyes."
And they told him,
    "Get in the boat.

"You'll hear gravel sounding.
    you'll know we've arrived.
"Then you can open your eyes.
"But if you open them before,
    we won't get there.
"We'll float right back here."
—"All right, I'll do that."

And so they paddled off,
    they told Coyote,
        "Lie face down in the boat!"
So Coyote lay face down.
So they paddled off.
Finally he got tired,
    Coyote did,
        lying face down.
And he thought,
    Coyote thought,
        "I'm going to peek out!"
Then when he peeked out,
    right then they floated ashore,
        at the shore of the ocean.
Then they told him,
    Coyote,
        "Now you won't go with us again."
And Coyote said,
    "This time I won't do it again, Nephew."
—"All right, let's go."

So Coyote went with them again.
And finally he had kept his eyes closed for a long ways.
Suddenly they paddled ashore.
And they said,
    "We've arrived."
And then he jumped up,

> Coyote did.
> And then he said,
>   "My country!"

A myth from the Keresan pueblos of New Mexico relates that, for his gluttony, Coyote was condemned to be a perpetual wanderer (Tyler 1975). Snyder paraphrases a type of passage that occurs in many narratives: "And [Coyote] sort of pulls himself back together and goes around and looks for a couple of his ribs that have kind of drifted down the hill, and pulls himself together and says, 'Well, now I'm going to keep on traveling'" (1977:72). The trickster figure in general has been characterized by Radin as having "an uncontrollable urge to wander" (1972:165), and by Ricketts as "a restless wanderer on the face of the earth" (1965:327). Contemporary poets, both Anglo and Native American, have also noted Coyote's nomadism. As Eugene Anderson writes, "The coyote nature is to travel forever" (1965:29). The Pueblo poet Simon Ortiz sees Coyote on Route 66, "just trucking along" (1977:15–18).

▼▼▼
TELLING ABOUT COYOTE

[From *A Good Journey*, by SIMON ORTIZ.]

> Old Coyote . . .
> "If he hadn't looked back
> everything would have been okay
> . . . like he wasn't supposed to,
>   but he did,
> and as soon as he did, he lost all his power,
> his strength."

". . . you know, Coyote
is in the origin and all the way
through . . . he's the cause
of the trouble, the hard times
that things have . . ."

"Yet, he came so close
to having it easy.
            But he said,
'Things are just too easy . . .'"
Of course he was mainly bragging,
shooting his mouth.
The existential Man,
Dostoevsky Coyote.

"He was on his way to Zuni
to get married on that Saturday,
and on the way there
he ran across a gambling party.
A number of other animals were there.
            He sat in
for a while, you know, pretty sure
of himself, you know like he is,
sure that he would win something.
                        But he lost
everything. Everything.
And that included his skin, his fur
which was the subject of envy
of all the other animals around."

"Coyote had the prettiest,
the glossiest, the softest fur
that ever was. And he lost that.
            So some mice
finding him shivering in the cold

beside a rock felt sorry for him.
'This poor thing, beloved,'
they said, and they got together
just some old scraps of fur
and glued them on Coyote with pinon pitch."

"And he's had that motley fur ever since.
You know, the one that looks like
scraps of an old coat, that one."

Coyote, old man, wanderer,
where you going, man?
Look up and see the sun.
Scorned, an old raggy blanket
at the back of the closet nobody wants.

"At this one conference
of all the animals there was a bird
with the purest white feathers.
His feathers were like, ah . . .
like the sun was shining on it
all the time but you could look at it
and you wouldn't be hurt by the glare.
It was easy and gentle to look at.
And he was Crow.
He was sitting at one side of the fire.
And the fire was being fed large pine logs,
and Crow was sitting downwind
from the fire, and the wind was blowing
that way . . .
            And Coyote was there.
He was envious of Crow because
all the other animals were saying,
'Wowee, look at that Crow, man,

just look at him,' admiring Crow.
Coyote began to scheme.
He kept on throwing pine logs into the fire,
ones with lots of pitch in them.
And the wind kept blowing,
all night long . . .
          Let's see,
the conference was about deciding
the seasons—when they should take place—
and it took a long time to decide that . . .
And when it was over, Crow was covered
entirely with soot. The blackest soot
from the pine logs.
And he's been like that since then."

"Oh yes, that was the conference
when Winter was decided
that it should take place
when Dog's hair got long.
              Dog said,
'I think Winter should take place
when my hair gets long.'
And it was agreed that it would. I guess
no one else offered a better reason."

        Who?
        Coyote?
O,
O yes, last time . . .
when was it,
I saw him somewhere
between Muskogee and Tulsa,
heading for Tulsy Town I guess,
just trucking along.

He was heading into some oakbrush thicket,
just over the hill was a creek.
Probably get to Tulsa in a couple days,
drink a little wine,
tease with the Pawnee babes,
sleep beside the Arkansas River,
listen to the river move,
. . . hope it don't rain,
hope the river don't rise.
He'll be back. Don't worry.
He'll be back.

Coyote's mobility seems easily relatable to both his eternal cu-
riosity and his scavenging nature. Biological research is consis-
tent with the mythic and literary traditions: coyotes have their
home burrows, but may range widely. In a study by R. D. An-
drews and E. K. Boggess, sixty-three coyotes were tagged, then
recovered over a four-year period. The straight-line distance
from the location where they were originally tagged was 22.2
miles; however, "male coyote movements ranged from 0 to 110
miles . . . and females ranged from 0 to 202 miles" (1978:261).

▼ COYOTE THE BRICOLEUR

Writers such as Radin and Ricketts have emphasized that the North American trickster frequently is also a transformer and culture-hero, whose accomplishments may include the slaying of monsters, the theft of natural resources for the benefit of man, the teaching of cultural skills, and the ordaining of laws. Yet the trickster is not an ideal heroic type: If he slays monsters, it is through guile rather than bravery. He does not create the world of the First People, but rather "fixes it up" so that it becomes the world of humanity. Thus, Ricketts calls him the "trickster-fixer" (1965:327). Ramsey rejects the term "culture-hero" and applies the Lévi-Straussian conception of bricoleur (1983: 41–42), "a sort of mythic handy-man who 'cobbles' reality in the form of a *bricolage* out of the available material" (35, 41).

▼▼▼
COYOTE AND FRIENDS

[Excerpt from *Reading the Fire*, by JAROLD RAMSEY.]

Perhaps at least a partial explanation is already before us. Just as the Trickster's dual role cannot be understood in terms of comparisons with Prometheus and other heroic benefactors in Western culture, so it cannot be understood in terms of Judeo-Christian ideas of "perfect origins," divine cosmogonies, and the like. Both the traditional literature and the native commentary upon it seem to validate, for Western tribes at least, Lévi-Strauss's conception of the Trickster-Transformer as a *bricoleur*, a sort of mythic handy-man who "cobbles" reality in the form of a *bricolage* out of the available material, and with something distinctly less transcendent than a divine plan or teleology to guide him—namely, his own impressionable, wayward, *avid* mind. To believe that the world as we have it is largely the work of a trickster is, in a mode of thought unfamiliar to our culture, to know and accept it *on its own terms*, neither postlapsarian nor millennial: as if to say, "Well, now, the world is not perfect; how could it be, given its original artisan, our trickster ancestor—but it's pretty good, considering; good enough, anyway. It's a world: ours." Or, in this judicious appraisal by a Thompson River Indian: "Coyote taught the people how to eat, how to wear clothes, make houses, hunt, fish, etc. Coyote did a great deal of good, but he did not finish everything properly. Sometimes he made mistakes, and although he was wise and powerful, he did many foolish things. He was too fond of playing tricks for his own amusement. He was also selfish, boastful, and vain."

As we have seen, one of the distinguishing properties of tricksters is their sheer vitality. Speaking of his long traffic as a poet with Coyote lore, Gary Snyder [1977:81] has remarked how "the first thing that excited me about Coyote tales was the delightful Dadaistic energy, leaping somehow into a modern frame of reference." That tricksters are overcharged with biological energy is dramatized of course in their overt actions as imaginative characters, given to trying *anything*; and it is also frequently expressed in casual supererogatory transformations of parts of their bodies into foodstuffs for the sustenance of the people to come. The feces of the Tillamook character "South Wind," for example, are turned into salmon-berries; portions of Wakdjunkaga's penis, when it is finally cut down to proper size, become staple roots and berries for the Winnebagos.

Tricksters are also, as we have noticed in passing, unkillable. They may suffer bad luck or just retribution in the form of starvation, poisoning, dismemberment, ingestion by monsters, incineration, drowning, fatal falls, and so on— but, as we would have it, it is a universal convention that they revive (either in explicit, generally formulaic episodes of revival, or implicitly, between one story and another), and go blithely on their way. They are mythic survivors, "hot for the world" (as Charles Olson once said of the Mayans) in a way that signifies, *per speculum mentis*, both the persistence in us of the unreconstructed Id, and the sheer avid amoral persistence of the human race itself. Trickster's lesson on this point is that the two things are profoundly interrelated.

In this role, Coyote has so much responsibility for our world that he is sometimes said to be "the Indian God" (De Angulo 1953:29). The Miwok say that Coyote destroyed the models which the other First People suggested for humanity, substituting a model that would have his own "cunning and adaptability" (Leydet 1977:78–79). For the Northern Paiute, Coyote is the inventor of sexual intercourse, as retold by Ramsey (1973:22).

▼▼▼
HOW HER TEETH WERE PULLED

[From *Love in an Earthquake*, by JAROLD RAMSEY.]

A Northern Paiute Myth (after Kelly)

In the old time women's cunts had teeth in them.
It was hard to be a man then
watching your squaw squat down to dinner
hearing the little rabbit bones crackle.

Whenever fucking was invented it died with the inventor.
If your woman said she felt like biting you didn't take it
  lightly.
Maybe you just ran away to fight Numuzoho the Cannibal.

Coyote was the one who fixed things,
he fixed those toothy women!
One night he took Numuzoho's lava pestle
to bed with a mean woman
and hammer hammer crunch crunch ayi ayi
all night long—
"Husband, I am glad," she said
and all the rest is history.
To honor him we wear our necklaces of fangs.

It is also often Coyote who institutes the elaborate taboos that
surround such activities as hunting and fishing. But the taboos
are not always original with him: sometimes they are pre-
existing. Then it is Coyote's role, in his bungling way, to discover
the taboos by breaking them. In a long myth of the Clackamas
Chinook (Boas 1894), of which only an excerpt is given below,
Coyote eventually learns all the taboos with the help of his "ass-
hole advisers": the talking turds that he voids and that he asks
for advice whenever he is perplexed. Finally all the taboos are
mastered, and Coyote can say: "This is how people will do."

▼ ▼ ▼

COYOTE ESTABLISHES FISHING TABOOS

[Told in Clatsop Chinook by CHARLES CULTEE. Translated with
FRANZ BOAS. Adapted by WILLIAM BRIGHT.]

Coyote was coming,
    he came to Got'at.

Now there was big surf,
    right away he went up to the spruce trees.

Now Coyote was afraid,
    he might get washed away,
    he stayed a long time at Got'at.
He took sand,
    he threw it in that surf.
"It will be a prairie,
    it will not be surf.
"Generations to come will walk on this prairie."
Now Clatsop became a prairie,
    that surf became a prairie.[1]

Now a creek came into being at Niakhaqshe.
He went,
    Coyote made a house at Niakhaqshe,
    he stood at the creek mouth of Niakhaqshe.
He speared two silverside salmon,
    he speared a steelhead,
    he speared a fall salmon.
He threw away that steelhead,
    he threw away that fall salmon.
"The creek is too small.
"I don't like its steelhead,
    I don't like its fall salmon.
"The creek is too small.
"It will be a bad omen,
    when a fall salmon is caught here,
    a person will die.
"Likewise a steelhead,
    when a female steelhead is caught,
    a woman will die,
    when a male steelhead is caught,
    a man will die.

"So it will be for the steelhead,
    so it will be for the fall salmon."

Now he picked up only those silversides,
    he went home.
Right away he cut them up,
    right away he steamed them,
    he ate them.
Day came,
    he took his spear,
    he went and stood at the creek mouth of Niakhaqshe.
He saw nothing,
    the floodtide set in,
    he went home.
Again daylight came,
    again he went,
    he went and stood there.
Again he saw nothing,
    he got angry,
    he went home.
He took a shit,
    he said to his shit,
    "Tell me,
    why have those silversides disappeared?"

"Oh, you have no sense,
    you bandylegs!
"When silversides are caught,
    when they are first caught,
    they must not be cut up.
"They must be split along the back,
    then they are roasted,
    they are not steamed.
"When they go upriver to the creeks,
    then they are steamed."

[Each day something similar happens. Coyote goes fishing and catches nothing. His shit insults him, and tells him about additional taboos that he has violated. Finally he succeeds in spearing ten silversides.]

Now he made spits,
   he made many spits.
Now he stayed awake,
   he roasted all he had caught.
Now he observed the taboos,
   the taboos of the silversides,
   when they first arrive at Niakhaqshe.
Then he stayed there,
   Coyote said,
   "So the people will do.
"If a corpse-handler eats silversides,
   right away they will disappear.
"If a murderer eats silversides,
   right away they will disappear.
"So also a menstruating girl,
   so also a menstruating woman."

[Coyote moves from Niakhaqshe to Clatsop and tries fishing again. The first day he catches two salmon with a net, and in the process he jumps over the net. The next day he catches nothing.]

Coyote was angry,
   he took a shit,
   he consulted his shit,
   he said, "You lied to me!"

"You bandylegs!
When people catch salmon,
   they mustn't jump over the net,
   you don't step across your net.

When the first salmon are caught,
   then they're cut up in the afternoon."

[On following days, Coyote again catches nothing. He learns about other taboos he has broken and, finally, he is able to catch fish again. But then he moves from Clatsop to another site. He catches a few fish on the first day, but nothing on the second day. His shit tells him, "Oh Coyote, you fool! Do you think it's the same here as at Clatsop?" Finally Coyote learns all the taboos, and he says:]

"So the people will do.
They will not catch salmon
   if they are murderers,
   corpse-handlers,
   menstruating girls,
   menstruating women,
   widowed people.
Those are all the taboos,
   for the generations to come."

Many stories tell how Coyote tinkers with the Eden of the original creator, or sabotages the noble intentions of a heroic figure, to make a world appropriate for humans who will be as imperfect as Coyote himself. A Karuk story explains why men and women were each given their tasks, "so they wouldn't be lazy" (Bright and Reuben 1982).

▼▼▼
COYOTE LAYS DOWN THE LAW

[Told in Karuk by NETTIE REUBEN. Translated with WILLIAM BRIGHT.]

People once said,
   "Let the river flow DOWNstream on one side,

and UPstream on the other side,
    let it be that way."
So all right,
    when they traveled DOWNstream by boat,
        they drifted down,
            downstream.
But they'd travel back up on the other side of the river,
    they'd drift upstream too,
        as it flowed UPstream,
            that water.

And then Coyote said,
    "Not at all!
        Let it not be that way,
            let it all flow DOWNstream.
"Let the young husbands have to push their way up there,
    when they travel UPstream."

And then again people said,
    "Women carry their packbaskets UPhill,
        up there they put wood in them,
            they make basketloads.
"Then the women leave for home.
"And they just leave them there,
    those basketloads."
And they said,
    "They'll just WALK home,
        those basketloads."

And then Coyote said,
    "Don't do that!
        Not at all!
            Let the young wives just CARRY the loads."
So that's how it is,
    now they don't walk any more,
        those basketloads.

It has sometimes been claimed that American Indian myths reflect a primarily male outlook; certainly Coyote's erotic adventures, which we will sample below, could be taken as supporting this. However, the stories were told on winter nights by both men and women, and occasionally a story seems to reflect a specifically female viewpoint. Thus the Southern Paiute relate how Coyote invented childbirth—and not by simply ordaining it, but by actually experiencing it (Sapir 1930:276–296).

▼▼▼
COYOTE GIVES BIRTH

[Told in Southern Paiute by TONY TILLOHASH. Translated with EDWARD SAPIR. Adapted by WILLIAM BRIGHT.]

> Coyote was living there, it is said,
>   and his wife said to him,
>   "Go get squaw-bush twigs for me,
>   I'm going to make a gathering-basket,
>   I say,
>   out of them."
> "Yes," said Coyote.
>
> Then he went off toward his squaw-bush,
>   he was very far along,
>   when he heard singing.
> "Oh!" said Coyote,
>   "It seems I'm getting power,
>   I'm almost having a dream,
>   I'm already a medicine man."
> Now he stood and listened,
>   he didn't hear it.
> Then he started off,

and he heard it again,
and it stopped again.

Then he stood and listened to it again,
he heard it well,
now he heard many people singing.
"We're traveling in order to eat people,"
they said,
singing along under the sky,
flying along,
those geese;
there were two chiefs,
one at each end,
as they traveled,
Coyote saw them.
Then he said,
"All the camping places,
those with springs,
those with mountains,
those with divides,
those with knolls,
those with valleys,
I know all their people.
"Go ahead and make me like you,
then I'll lead you,"
said Coyote.
"What did Coyote say?"
said they,
asking each other.
"He knows them all,
he says,
the lands where we're going."
Then that chief of theirs said,
"Let that Coyote talk,

he's not a good one,
 he'll give us away."

Coyote ran along under them,
 shouting as he went.
"Oh," said the chief,
 "doing like that,
 he might get us caught.
"Let's each give him feathers,"
 said the chief.
Then they flew down onto Coyote,
 Coyote kept dodging,
 but they each gave him feathers.
They told Coyote,
 "Go ahead and fly to that little ridge,
 then come back."
"Yes," said Coyote,
 and flew off,
 he flew beyond the little ridge.
"What did I say?"
 said the chief,
 "That Coyote will always be that way,
 he won't obey us."
Coyote came back from beyond the little ridge,
 he reached them.
Then that chief said,
 "You won't keep flying around us,
 you won't shout,
 you won't sing loudly."
"Yes," said Coyote.

They all started to fly toward the sky.
Then they flew westward,
 wherever they were bound,
 Coyote flew back and forth around them.

Then the chief said,
  "Let's pull out his feathers,
  he'll give us away."
Then they grabbed him under the sky,
  they took off his feathers,
  Coyote went plunging down,
  he fell on the ground,
  he lay senseless.
Then pretty soon he came to,
  he saw some mush.
"Oh!" he said,
  "It seems my friends gave me some mush,"
  said he as he ate it.

Then pretty soon,
  when he finished eating it,
  he felt a cold chill go through his head.
Then he touched his head.
"Oh!" said Coyote,
  "Is it my own brains I've been eating?"
He tried to vomit,
  Coyote was angry.
"Let me follow their tracks."
Coyote traveled westward,
  he camped several nights on the way.

Then pretty soon he heard them,
  singing as they traveled.
"Coyote," they said,
  "There in the midst of the people
  lies the woman you like."
"Yes," said Coyote.
There in that camp,
  there he arrived,
  he looked for the woman,

he managed to find her.
"So what shall I do to her?"
    said Coyote.
He got on top of her,
    he began to stamp on her stomach,
    as he did that to her,
    that baby fell out.

"So what shall I do with it?"
    said Coyote.
Then he swallowed it,
    he came back toward his own country,
    again he camped several nights on the way,
    he had a stomach ache.
"That's how it will be with a woman,"
    said Coyote.
Then he heated stones in the fire,
    after that he hung on to a cedar limb,
    as he did so the baby fell down.
Then he went far off
    and got an armful of wood,
    he got back,
    built a fire,
    he lay on the stones he'd heated,
    he drank warm water.
Then he made a head-scratcher,
    he scratched his head with it.
"This is what a woman will do
    when she gives birth to a child,"
    so said Coyote.

Perhaps most momentous of all, Coyote is, for many tribes, the inventor of death. Some California tribes relate that "Earth-maker" wanted to give people eternal life, but Coyote invented death "to make people take life more seriously." Elsewhere, he

oresees that death will be necessary to prevent overpopulation.
When his own child dies, he wants to revoke the rule, but by
then it is too late; Coyote becomes the first to feel the bereave-
ment which is to be the lot of humanity.[2] (We will see the details
in chapter 11.)

Coyote's character as bricoleur seems to be a function of his
inquisitiveness and his reckless willingness to give anything a
try. Among the Hopi, Coyote is assigned a Pandora-like role.
His curiosity makes him open the jar in which the stars are
hoarded up, letting them escape into the sky—but he is too im-
patient to arrange them systematically (Tyler 1975:164–165).

▼▼▼
COYOTE PLACES THE STARS

[Excerpt from *Pueblo Animals and Myths*, by HAMILTON TYLER.]

Coyote continues his cosmic bungling in the company of
the Twins [a pair of divine boys], this time in a Hopi ac-
count of placing the stars. He is no deity here but a scape-
goat. When the people emerged from the Underworld it
was dark, so they made stars and told the War Twins to go
place them properly. "Coyote said to himself, 'I will go with
the two boys.' They put the seven together, the Pleiades, in
a good position, and those six, Orion, they put them to-
gether, and the biggest one they put toward the east, and
another they put on the south side, and another on the west
side, and another on the north side. Then they put up the
dipper."

It will be noted that the ceremonial circuit which usually
goes from north to west, or counterclockwise, is here re-
versed. "Just when they had put all these up, Coyote said to
himself, 'It is a big job!' He said to the boys, 'We shall never

finish this work, we shall all die first, why can't we do this?'
And he took the stars and threw them in every direction,
improperly." The next night the Evening Star came out in
its place and by and by the others that had been properly
positioned. "Then they saw stars scattered all over the sky.
The people said, 'Bad Coyote, you did that?'—'Yes,' he
said.—'If you had not gone with them, all the stars would
be well placed. But you are bad Coyote; you scattered them
all over the sky.' They were very angry. But Coyote said,
'That's all right, it's a lot of work to put them all into good
positions, better to scatter them around.'"

All the traits of Old Man Coyote that have been mentioned—
and those to be mentioned later, too—are summed up by Dell
Hymes (1978) in a paean which must break a record for number
of footnotes per line of verse:

▼▼▼

FIVEFOLD FANFARE FOR COYOTE

[By DELL HYMES.]

> unwearied, unweathered, unwashed, unwished,   I
>   unworshiped—
> wily wencher, wiver, widower, waif—
> whimsical whiffler, whistler, wheedling whangam—
> wayfarer, wangler, welsher, wastrel, wallower—
> walking, watching, warning, warding, warranting—
>
> *mousing, mating, mischieving, metamorphosing!*
> *malingering, mimicking, miscible mirror!*
> *Misogynist—Mongrel—Munchausen—Minister—Muse!*
>
> fooling friends, foiling foes, featly transforming fiends &
> finagling, fingering, fucking, forsaking females &
> fixing flora & fauna in future functions &

fabricating facilely, foraging fortunately, famously
Fecund Factotum—
    Fornicating Physician—
        FOUNDER!

befuddled, besmirched, beleaguered, belittled begetter—
profane, prophylactic, prolix, procrustean precursor—

        WANDERER   II
        MISCREANT
        FORNICATOR
        BUNGLER
        PRONOUNCER—

        IT'ÁLAP'AS!   III
        TÉNIQ'ÍYA! STANK'IYA!
        ISK'ÚLYA!
        ÉSHIN! ASHNÍ!
        SPILYÁI!

never will he go from this land,   IV
    here always, as long as the land is,
    that is how Coyote is in this land
    (Coyote, surviving all names);
    now I know only that far.....

The people coming are near now.....
Story! Story!

        In the sunshine, in the sunshine,   V
        All kinds of butterflies flying around!
        No flies!

    Notes on Fivefold Fanfare for Coyote

I & II.
Suggestions for orchestration
    Any or all of the following in the appropriate
    sections, lines:

1. [w]: windchime, woodwind choir, whip, whistle, ukelele, oboe.
2. [m]: marimba, mandolin (of any kind), maraca, monochord=manichord (=clavichord), mellowphone (an althorn in circular form).
3. [f]: flute, French horn, fiddle (country style), finger cymbals.
4. [b]: bassoon, bass viol, banjo, bass drum, bass clarinet, blocks, brass wind choir.
5. [p]: piccolo, piano, percussion section.

No specification for the Indian names of Coyote and the last lines. Perhaps shouted? at least the names? and last lines sung without accompaniment?

A note on the appropriateness of the scheme of sounds:

In Chinookan labial consonants are less numerous and frequent than consonants of other kinds (dentals, palatals, velars). Considerably less so: a trait shared with some other North Pacific Coast languages, also with few labial stops.

p~b alternate in most dialects, and in most positions in Wasco.

b~m have alternated in Lower Chinook (cf. Gibbs, Boas on difficulty of distinguishing the two sounds).

m~w have alternated between dialects (cf. -utxix, -mtxix; -uča, -mča).

f is not found at all as a regular sound; occurs once in Wishram Texts as the sound [fu:] of the sucking monster with whom Coyote has one of his adventures; probably an ingressive [f] (hence an inversion of normal f).

Hence, in mutability, marginality, mirroring (inversely) of normal, the labial order of consonants is the appropriate one, Chinookan-wise, for Coyote.

III.

Isk'úlya: Wasco name for Coyote (Wasco, Wishram).

It'álap'as: principal name for Coyote among the other Chinookans (Clackamas, Kathlamet, Shoalwater, Clatsop); known to other Oregon groups, such as Tillamook, and perhaps used (not able to check Tillamook here). Known and used in Wishram Texts.

Éshin: name for Coyote among Tualatin branch of the Kalapuya, including the Yamhill; recorded in phonetically variant forms by Gatschet, Frachtenberg, De Angulo, Jacobs (collated by Henry Zenk).

Ashní: name for Coyote among the Santiam branch of the Kalapuya; as recorded by Jacobs from John Hudson.

Spilyái: name for Coyote as person in myths among Sahaptins (Warm Springs, Yakima, Umatilla), still surviving in daily use.

IV & V.

The full set of possible elements of an ending of a myth seems to include, in both Chinookan and Sahaptin, five things.

1. the end of the immediate action.

2. pronouncements, transformations, what the people will say, what animals will do, including reference to 'the people who are coming are near now.'

3. (sometimes) a remark implying that the myth world itself continued beyond the myth (Now I know only that far, I do not know where he went from there).

4. formal end to the story itself (k'ani k'ani with Mrs. Howard, and sometimes in Wasco/Kathlamet; usually qédau iqánuck 'Thus the myth' with Louis Simpson).

5. (sometimes) an invocation/announcement? of good weather (seeming to show the ritual efficacy of the myth telling, as a world maintenance/renewal activity); (once in

Mrs. Howard: 'Hurry! Summer! Grouse are hooting!');
(frequent with Cultee: 'Tomorrow good/fine weather'
[apparently literally] 'Tomorrow very-very-clear').

IV.

A composite of lines from endings: 'The people who are
coming are near now,' 'Now I know only that far,' 'Story,
story!' from Mrs. Victoria Howard. 'Never will he go from
this land, always, as long as the land is' and 'That is how
Coyote is in the land' are taken from Jacobs, Northwest Sa-
haptin Texts (Columbia University Contributions to An-
thropology, volume XIX, Parts I, II) (New York, 1937) (Re-
printed New York: AMS Press, 1969), the English on p. 57
in I, the Sahaptin (Klickitat) p. 50 in II. It's a moving end-
ing, how Coyote, getting to the land of the dead (near the
sun) is sent back by a higher power. The first two quoted
lines are translated more literally here, by me.

V.

The last three lines are the English version of the ending of
a story told by Susan Moses of Warm Springs, in Sahaptin,
a literal translation except that there are some additional
particles in the first line that defy rendition, though stated
to be integral to the conventional ending by another Sahap-
tin speaker. (Their meanings are of the effect, 'and,' 'now,'
'indeed'; the main word in the line is literally 'it-sunshines').

What can be said about *Canis latrans* as bricoleur? The bio-
logical connection seems to lie in the elements of curiosity and
cunning, for which anecdotal evidence is abundant. Thus, Ley-
det refers to the coyote's "unsleeping desire to investigate any-
thing unusual" (1977:44); Ryden quotes an ex-trapper as saying
that coyotes "are the smartest animals in the world" (1975:4).
The zoological literature seems to say little about coyote intel-
ligence as such, though the animal's keen and versatile percep-

ual abilities are noted. P. N. Lehner observes that the design of the coyote eye allows the animal to be active both by night and by day (1978:129). Bekoff remarks that coyotes are well adapted for hunting by the combined use of sight, hearing, and smell (1978:118). Leydet cites an Indian saying that "a feather fell from the sky . . . the eagle saw it, the deer heard it, the bear smelled it, the coyote did all three" (1977:56).

A possible biological explanation for the coyote's inquisitiveness and cunning is offered by Ryden in terms of the fact that young coyotes remain dependent on their parents for a relatively long period—a phenomenon called *neoteny*, displayed most strikingly by humans (1975:250–251). As she puts it, "Neoteny is a characteristic of all species that have not inherited a fixed repertory of behavior, but must *learn* how to survive. . . . The neotenal coyote . . . meets change by learning new responses and is therefore capable of developing a whole new lifestyle" (1975:250–251). The suggestion is that coyotes have gone beyond their canid brothers, the dogs and wolves—as humans have gone beyond their primate kindred—in their motivation and ability to learn, and have thereby increased their adaptability—a signal quality that will be discussed below.[3]

6 ▼ COYOTE THE GLUTTON

Being a typical trickster, Coyote is widely portrayed as voracious, indeed omnivorous; though he may promise to restrain his appetite, he always gives in. The Karuk story-cycle that describes his travel upriver to get money contains a whole sequence of episodes regarding Coyote's appetite. First he gets thirsty and steals Lizard's gooseberry juice (Bright 1980b:27–29).

▼ ▼ ▼
COYOTE STEALS A DRINK

[Told in Karuk by JULIA STARRITT. Translated with WILLIAM BRIGHT.]

> So Coyote hurried upstream.
> And he traveled a long time.
> And he got thirsty,
>   VERY thirsty.
> And his tongue was very dry.
> And he saw a sweathouse was standing there.
> And he saw a man was sweating himself there,
>   he was singing.
> And Coyote was terribly thirsty.
> And he saw two baskets of gooseberry juice there.

And he said, "Good!
    I'll drink Nephew's juice.
"I'll just take a little taste!"
And again,
    "I have to drink just a little more!"
And he drank up both bowls.
And he said, "Nephew,
    you mustn't be angry at me!"
And then he hurried upstream.

.ut Lizard curses Coyote, and causes him to eat a tabooed food
Bright 1980b:27–29).

▼▼▼
OYOTE EATS GRASSHOPPERS

Told in Karuk by CHESTER PEPPER. Translated with WILLIAM
RIGHT.]

And so when Lizard came out,
    came out of the sweathouse,
        then he thought, "Ah!
            I bet Coyote's been around here!
"He's drunk up that juice of mine.
"May he be thirsty!"
And he thought,
    "He likes those things,
        roasted grasshoppers."
And he said,
    "May there be a brushfire,
        up ahead of him!"[1]

Coyote went on upstream,
    there had been a big brushfire.

And he looked around,
   there were lots of roasted grasshoppers.
"I won't eat them."
Finally he went a little ways.
And he thought,
   "I'll just gather a few of them,
     those roasted grasshoppers."
There he was going to gather them.
And then he thought,
   "I wonder why it is,
     I'm not getting full."
And he thought,
   "I think they're coming out my rear,
     while I'm eating them."
And he thought,
   "I'll plug up my ass!"
So he gathered pitch,
   and he plugged up his ass with it.
And he thought, "There,
   now I'll get full.
I've plugged up my ass."

So he ate them—
   but there had been a BIG brushfire.
And he was sticking his butt all around there.
And he thought,
   "I think I'm getting there,
    to Klamath Falls"—
     he heard it,
      the thundering,
       he heard it like that,
        it sort of said HUHUHUHUHU.
And he thought,

"I'm getting there,
    to Klamath Falls"—
        all he could hear was that HUHUHUHUHU.
It was really his ass,
    there it was burning.
It was really the pitch,
    what he had plugged it with,
        there it was burning.
What could he do?
He slid all around there,
    on the ground, in the sand.
And he was just saying "ATUHTUHTUHTUHTUH!"
So finally his ass stopped burning.
And he thought,
    "Now I'll never eat them again,
        those roasted grasshoppers.
That's enough, I won't eat them!"

But now the rest of Lizard's curse—that Coyote should become thirsty—comes into effect. Because Coyote is on a wealth quest, he is not supposed to drink water at all; furthermore, each time he approaches a creek, it magically dries up. Even when he stands at a distance and throws his blanket in the creek bed, "only dust puffs up, / the water has gone dry." Finally Coyote resorts to drinking from the Klamath River, although drinking river water is absolutely taboo. He falls into the river, "drowns," and washes away downstream—only to have more adventures of both gluttony and lechery.

In a story from the Cupeño of Southern California (Hill and Nolasquez 1973:60–61), Coyote goes even further in breaking taboos. To cover up his ineptitude as a hunter, he becomes a cannibal, but then is haunted by his victim's ghost. This is surely a tale told to frighten children at the dark of the moon.

▼▼▼
COYOTE COOKS HIS DAUGHTER

[Told in Cupeño by ROSINDA NOLASQUEZ. Translated with JANE H. HILL. Adapted by WILLIAM BRIGHT.]

So Coyote was there,
   and his daughter,
   just one was there.
And their brush house stood at the foot of the mountain.
And there they were.
And then Coyote said,
   they had no food put away.
And Coyote went hunting,
   he fetched his bow.
And he went,
   he took his daughter.

So he kept circling around in a wash,
   his tail went switch-switch-switch,
   gallop-gallop-gallop he went,
   he kept coming along running.
And his daughter kept coming slowly behind him.
So Coyote look-look-looked behind him,
   his ears he twitch-twitch-twitched.
And he kept coming, coming, coming,
   he was jump-jump-jumping,
   he trot-trot-trotted.

So there at the mountain they arrived.
And there he kept walking around,
   he would go looking for something to eat.
So he kept jumping,
   he would catch an ant.

And he kept coming, coming, coming,
   they arrived there.

So there was a lake there,
   there he drank water.
So his daughter kept coming behind him.
So she kept coming slowly,
   Coyote kept jump-jump-jumping,
   his tail went switch-switch-switch,
   he look-look-looked behind him,
   he turn-turn-turned his head,
   he shook-shook-shook-shook his head.
So he kept coming.
And his wife was there at home.

So she was gathering all the grass,
   to cook something for him there.

And then it was evening.
And Coyote saw nothing there.
So he didn't see anything to kill.
So grabbing his daughter,
   he hit her with a stick.
So it was a pine stick,
   the stick.
And he killed that daughter of his.
And from there he carried her home on his back,
   he came.

So he kept slowly coming along,
   dragging his tail.
So he arrived there,
   his wife was there by the door of the brush house.
And he arrived there.

So then he took all that hair off his daughter.
And there was a big place for cooking
 something in the way of food,
 he cut up his daughter there,
 Coyote did.
And he cooked her.
So he boil-boil-boiled it,
 her meat.
And he licked his hand like this,
 he took it out,
 he kept lick-licking it.
And he boiled it,
 it got real green.

And then she came from there,
 his daughter.
And she spoke,
 as she came,
 "Pine tree, stick,
 pine tree, grass stick
 jingle-ingle-ingle."
And still she came.
And her mother was there by the door.
And the girl's beads went,
 "Jingle-jingle-jingle."
And she said,
 "Pine tree, stick,
 pine tree, grass stick
 jingle-ingle-ingle."

So the mother looked around,
 she looked,
 Coyote was still there cooking,
 the dust was still rising like this.
So he kept brushing his tail like this.

And the daughter was a ghost.
And she said,
    "Pine tree, stick,
    pine tree, grass stick
    jingle-ingle-ingle."
And her mother said,
    "Ah! it must be her voice I hear,
    it must be her,"
    she said.

"She's turned into a ghost,"
    she said.
"Pine tree, stick,
    pine tree, grass stick
    jingle-ingle-ingle."
"Well," said the woman,
    "this guy must have killed her already,
    and here he is walking around."

And she went around her house.
"Pine tree, stick,
    pine tree, grass stick
    jingle-ingle-ingle."
"Already she speaks to me,"
    said the woman,
"This guy must have killed her."

"And now for sure you come here to me,"
    said the woman,
    "and I'll burn you now."
So right then she got up,
    the old woman Coyote.
And she gathered all the grass,
    while Coyote was cooking his food.
And right away she fetched it.

And she burn-burn-burned everything.
So then their house went up in smoke.
And he said, "Oh,
   old woman, old woman,
   don't burn me, don't burn me!"
So all that house of theirs burned
And Coyote burned,
   he burned up.
And he died.

All this gluttonous behavior is, of course, typical of the trickster, who is described by Ricketts as "insatiably hungry"; he will "do anything to obtain a meal" (1965:327, 347). His greediness can, of course, be seen as one aspect of the "oral behavior" which Abrams and Sutton-Smith (1977:32) include in their inventory of trickster traits (Coyote is also an inveterate singer, talker, and braggart).

The natural history literature and scientific writings confirm that coyotes are scavengers and omnivores. According to a Western American saying, "A coyote will eat anything that doesn't eat him first." However, *Canis latrans* is apparently capable of much more restraint than his mythic counterpart; thus, Ryden has observed a coyote "freezing" for as long as eleven minutes when stalking a ground squirrel (1979:214). It appears that the impulsive aspect of Old Man Coyote's appetite, like some other features to be discussed below, is derived more from the human than from the quadruped side of his nature.

The insatiable and indiscriminate horniness of Coyote is well known. He copulates with married women, with virgins at their puberty rites, with his own daughter, and with crones (perhaps, like Don Giovanni, *delle vecchie fa conquista / pel piacer di porle in lista*). He is exceptionally proficient at getting his partners pregnant: in the Karuk cycle of "Coyote's Travels," after he has "drowned" in the river, he turns himself into a "pretty little piece of driftwood" to attract the attention of two girls (Bright 1980*b*:35–37).

▼▼▼
COYOTE TURNS INTO DRIFTWOOD

[Told in Karuk by NETTIE REUBEN. Translated with WILLIAM BRIGHT.]

So then he stooped to the water,
   he stooped a long time,
      down to the water,
         he drank a lot.
And when he got up,
   he'd drunk a lot.
There he fell over backwards,
   he fell backwards into the river.

And then he floated downriver.
Finally he floated a long ways back downstream.
Finally he floated back here to the center of the world.
And then he looked downriver.
There were young women downriver leaching flour,
   on the shore.
And then he said,
   "I'll turn into some pretty driftwood!"
And then he turned into some pretty driftwood.
And then he floated down from upstream,
   he watched them close by,
      while they were leaching flour.
And he said,
   "I'll float to the shore,
      I'll float to the shore!
"I'll keep floating in circles just downslope from them."
And then one girl looked downslope to the river.
And she said, "Look, my dear!
   Oh, look how pretty,
      downslope,
         that driftwood!"
And the other said, "Where?"
And the first said, "There, downslope."
And the other said, "Oh! my dear,
   let's hook it out,
      that driftwood!"
"All right!"
So they ran downslope,
   they went to look at it,
      where it was floating in circles.
And one said, "Come on, my dear,
   Where's a little stick?
"We'll hook it out with that."

And so they hooked it out.
And oh! they took a liking to it.
Oh, how pretty it was,
    the driftwood,
       they took a liking to it!
And then one threw it to another,
    they played with it,
       that driftwood,
          the pretty little stick.
And then one girl said, "Ugh!"
    she said, "Ugh! Maybe it's Coyote,
       they said he drowned in the river, upstream."
And then they threw it back in the river,
    that driftwood.
And they took it up,
    their acorn mush,
       what they were leaching.
Sure enough, in a while, they both were pregnant.
There Coyote floated downstream,
    then he floated ashore downriver from them.

Coyote's erotic exploits do not always turn out so well—but he is never discouraged for long. Consider William Brandon's "free" ethnopoetic version of a Cochití myth[1] (1971: 54–56).

▼▼▼
COYOTE AND BEAVER EXCHANGE WIVES

[Excerpt from *The Magic World*, by WILLIAM BRANDON.]

Old Coyote and Old Coyote Woman lived
on one side of the hill

Old Beaver and Old Beaver Woman lived on
the other side of the hill

One night it was snowing

I will invite my brother Beaver to go hunting
said Old Coyote

and whoever hunts the best will have the other's wife
said Old Coyote

So he went to see Old Beaver

> We'll go hunting and if we kill rabbits
> we'll bring them to our wives
> said Old Coyote

> I'll take mine to your wife and
> you take yours to my wife

Old Beaver smoked a while

> All right
> said Old Beaver

> You go first, since you invited me

> All right I will go in the morning
> said Old Coyote

> I will go hunting for you
> he said to Old Beaver Woman

> I will sing a song for you
> so you may kill many rabbits
> said Old Beaver Woman

So Old Coyote was gone all day hunting

In the evening Old Beaver Woman sang her song
        Old Coyote Old Coyote come and sleep with me
        Old Coyote Old Coyote come make love to me

Then she howled like a coyote
        Woo-wu!wu!wu!woooooo-wook-wike-yike-yiyiyiyi-
                woooooo-woo!

                He won't kill anything
                said Old Beaver

                He isn't any hunter
                It won't do you any good to sing

But Beaver woman waited and waited
singing and singing

But Old Coyote killed nothing at all
so he never appeared at all

The next day Old Beaver went hunting

He told Old Coyote Woman to wait for him
He told her he was going to kill rabbits for her

Then he hunted
and killed so many rabbits he could hardly carry them

and hardly able to carry them
he brought them to Coyote's house

        Old Coyote Woman, here are the rabbits

        Thank you thank you Old Man Beaver

They went straight into the inner
room and left Old Man Coyote by himself

Old Man Coyote was unhappy

They gave him his supper and then
they went in to bed

Old Beaver Man started putting his penis into
Old Coyote Woman and
Old Coyote Woman cried out and cried out at the
top of her voice

Old Beaver don't you hurt my wife
said Old Coyote

> Shut up Old Man Coyote
> said Coyote Woman
> I am crying out because I like it

> You old fool
> said Coyote Woman

When they were finished Old Beaver Man came out and
said to Old Coyote

> We won't have bad feelings
> you know this was your idea

So they all remained friends
the same as ever

Coyote is even capable of autofellation, as recounted in Dell
Hymes's translation of a Chinookan text (1981a:236–237).[2]

▼▼▼
COYOTE SUCKS HIMSELF

[Told in Clackamas Chinook by VICTORIA HOWARD. Translated with
MELVILLE JACOBS. Adapted by DELL HYMES.]

He went,
   he was going along,

now he thought:
    "I shall suck myself."
He went on,
    off the trail, he covered himself with five rocks,
      now there he stayed.
He sucked himself,
    he finished,
      he came out.

He was going along,
    he saw a canoe going downriver,
      he thought,
        "Let me inquire of them.
        "Perhaps something is news."
He hallooed to them;
    they heard him,
      they told him,
        "Ehhh what?"
He told them,
    "Isn't something news?"
    "Indeed. Come a little this way."
He went close to the river.
    "Yesss,"
      they told him;
        "Coyote was coming along,
          "now he covered himself with rocks.
        "He sucked himself.
        "Such is the news that's traveling along."
He thought,
    "Hmmm! Wonder who saw me?"

He went back,
    where he sucked himself at;
he saw,
    the rocks are split,

where the news had rushed out.
He thought:
  now he said:
  "Indeed,
    "even though it was I myself,
    "the news rushed out."
  "Now the people are near.
    "Whatever they may do,
    "should they suppose,
      "'No one will ever make me their news,'
    "out it will come."

Again, this is typical behavior for the trickster, who is "grossly erotic" (Ricketts 1965:327); his promiscuity can also be seen, in a somewhat larger context, as a manifestation of his "sheer vitality" (Ramsey 1983:41)—his "delightful Dadaistic energy," as Snyder says (1977:81). All this has been especially appealing to a number of modern poets, such as Bennett (1982:127).

▼▼▼

COYOTE IN LOVE

[By BRUCE BENNETT. Published in *Coyote's Journal*.]

"Sure I've done it
with other women
but you're the one
I'm always touching . . ."
So Coyote
tells his women
always the same
to all his women
who always believe him.
Or so he tells me.

Peter Blue Cloud, a poet of Iroquois origin, has written some
f the best Coyoterotica, with plots taken from Western Indian
aditions and his own imagination. In Blue Cloud's "Coyote
Ian and Saucy Duckfeather," the trickster plays the traditional
ple of the seducer who achieves his aims by pretending to give
namanistic treatment. Saucy Duckfeather is a flirtatious young
narried woman whose dream is to have pure white feathers;
oyote is the great doctor who promises to fulfill her wish. To
nis end he concocts a story about a "male tree" that can grant
vishes if it can only find its mate (1978:29–37).

▾▾▾
OYOTE MAN AND SAUCY DUCKFEATHER

From *Back Then Tomorrow*, by PETER BLUE CLOUD.]

of course they called her that because
of the way she moved her rump to some
secret music or itch, so proud she was,
married to White Crane Man whose every

feather was valued by those over-the-
water-people, sure she was pretty
and even the old men who helped gather
firewood, you seen them eyeing that tail

with their mouths like wrinkled holes,
and Young Singer, too, would hang around
the village and trip over everything
while pretending not to watch her:

yes, all the men and boys of age were
walking around on three legs and not
much fishing or hunting getting done,
not to mention some pretty jealous

women, like Bullhead Woman who took
some old duck feathers and stuck them up
her butt, and wiggle-walked all over camp,
saying loud, "how you like this, huh,

it look sassy enough for all you men?"
but Saucy Duckfeather wouldn't notice
any of these things, down by the shore
she was smoothing her feathers and

looking at herself in the water, and
wishing her secret longing that her
feathers might turn shiny white, and
then, what a gorgeous creature she

would become, a truly fitting
companion for the White Crane Man,
oh, what a pair like sunlight they
would be, and their children surely

shame the great swan so white: and
Magpie Woman was hopping all around
camp, picking up twigs for her
small campfire, and worried, too,

old woman that she was,
with no more men whose duty
was to give her meat of the hunt
and once in a while load of branches,

stirring her tiny basket of mush,
mumbling to herself these last
few weeks, and now, suddenly
reached her decision, and a very

hard one to reach, too, but
nothing else to be done, no,

it had to be, to call in that
crazy Coyote Man, so full of

tricks and mischief all the time and
never content to only gamble
with the men, but had to be
out in the brush chasing after

all those young women, and
now Magpie Woman sighed, and then
giggled in remembering her youth,
yes, yes, there always seemed to be

eager young women, way out
there, pretending to gather wood
or dig for food, the better to be
caught by Coyote Man or any other

like himself, for of course
there are many kinds of coyote,
among all men, not to mention
certain kinds of women, too,

who glory in mischief and hidden
games, among the bushes or in
the forest, but that's always
been so, sighed Magpie Woman

and giggled again in rememberance,
and "yes," she re-decided, "I will invite
Coyote Man to feast with me,
though I have little enough, but

little enough is often plenty for
those whose hunger is not always
stomach food," and anyway she'd
seen that Coyote Man often, yes,

when he'd come to doctor someone,
looking, studying that Saucy
Duckfeather and more, too, in his
eyes than just curious sparkles:

and so, pretending to be very sick she tore
her hair and cried that only Coyote Man
could cure her, and of course he heard
of it soon enough and was seen coming

down the hill with his basket on
his back and singing loud and long a
song which the young men envied
for it could not be imitated because

the hearer forgot it as soon as hearing
it, and only remembered the beauty of it, and
"oh, oh, here he comes again, and watch
out for everything you own and

especially watch out for wives,
daughters, nieces and any grandmothers,"
they said, and Coyote Man he
step-danced into camp and threw

his basket down, heavy with rocks
he pretended were beads, and right on
the foot of Badger's Son who screamed
in pain and danced around on the other

foot, and Coyote Man turned and looked
shocked, and studied the young man's
step, then declared, "well, it's a
fancy step all right, but I don't

think you'll win any girls with
it," which set the other men to

laughing, which good mood Coyote
Man needed to get about his business:

so he took up his basket and went to
the house of Magpie Woman and entered and
stood looking down at her for a long
time, then said, "well, well, yes I can see

that you're not sick at all and will
probably outlive youngsters," and smiled
at her and she smiled back, "you
look just like your father, you

surely do, and wherever did he go to?"
Coyote Man still smiling, "yes,
that old man left for upriver some
time back and I guess he found a

a good place to be," and of course it was
the very same Coyote Man because
in old age a coyote often gets
much younger, but secrets are to

keep and so, he asked her what her
problem was and she, she talked
while stirring him a basket of
mush and fed him the last of the

salmon, and he listened and nodded and
mumbled, "hmm, yes, I see; I got
lots of other important things to do,
but my father was your friend, so

I guess I can help you, yes, I
guess I'll do this thing just
for old times' sake, yes," and he
ate and had a nap to refresh his

mind and dreamed just the right
dream: so when Magpie Woman walked
from her house at sundown all cured, the
camp had a dance to celebrate this

miraculous cure by Coyote Man, and
the feet stomped all night and lots
of rustling and giggling in the
brush after Coyote Man hinted

to certain young women of
the power root he had obtained in
downriver country, which the women
there all used to be sure to have

male children, and this root was only
to be used at night of course and
attached to the front of a man
who knew the song that went with

it: and so Coyote Man slept all the
next day almost, and then faded
into the woods with some of
the salmon and beads brought to him by

grateful young women who were sure
now of male children, and Coyote
Man, when out of sight picked vines
and stripped the bark, and bent them

just like strings of moneybeads, for
of course he had only one real string
for his last night's work, and he filled
his burden basket with the vines

and placed the beads on top, and went
walking fast through the camp and

mumbling to himself so that all
could hear, "oh, these heavy beads

again, and I suppose there'll be more
there tomorrow night that I'll
have to carry away, oh, if I could
just give them all away instead," and

he threw the string of real beads to
some young men hanging around Saucy
Duckfeather, and kept right on going,
and next morning they saw him again,

walking real fast through the camp with
a basket full of salmon which
was really dyed pieces of bark
with a few real salmon on top

which he threw to the people
and mumbled that he wished he
could rest awhile and not have
to be always getting beads and

salmon and taking them from one
place to another, and the salmon
he threw landed pretty close
to Saucy Duckfeather, and so

she began to wonder about this
Coyote Man with so much wealth and
the only one around with no time
to look at her, and there he went,

disappearing into the brush, and then
again in the afternoon he re-appeared, and
this time he was carrying a great bundle
of white deer skins, but moving so fast

that the people could just make out
the one which hung loose, and he
once again disappeared until almost
dark, when he danced into camp,

his head and shoulders turned a
brilliant gold like the sun,
the brightest and most beautiful of
feathers ever seen around, and

eyes of greed, or wonder, or just
dreaming never know the truth of
pine pitch and yellow ocher and quick
motion in fading light: and now,

waiting, waiting, the snare was
set and the prey was curious, as
Saucy Duckfeather began, but
not to let anyone notice, of course,

following Coyote Man around and
he pretended not to notice her and
walked away from camp and looked
to the hills from which he'd come, and

holding his head as in great pain, he
moaned, "oh, I wish that tree would
just leave me alone, oh, where can
a simple man like myself find a

mate for the male tree? oh, I
know it's said that she'll appear
soon, and every wish of hers be granted,
but how will I know her to be

the one the male tree wishes and
how will I be able to tell that

she deserves to be the one? oh,
now that I'm wealthy and have

wished myself a hood and mantle
of golden feathers, still the
other tree cries out to me and
makes my head feel so much

pain, oh, I got to find that
woman for the male tree," and
Saucy Duckfeather did not even
hesitate, but said, "it's me,

the male tree has called me, and
I'm instructed to ask of you,
Coyote Man, what I must do
to have my wish of feathers white

as polished shell or snow, what
must I do?" and he jumped at
her voice, a man caught guilty
and looked at her a long while, yes,

thinking, just, oh yes, and "yes,"
he said, "perhaps you are the
one, and I guess I must tell you
the all of it so simple, merely

a tree, a male tree, a dead oak
with a protruding red branch near
the bottom which a woman must
mount and ride upon a four night

ride, an all night ride with
no time wasted, just riding and
wishing a four night journey
to bring about the truth of all

your dreams": and there was Coyote
Man standing inside the hollow oak,
his pecker sticking way out and
so hard his hide was stretched

toward the root of his manhood
that he couldn't even blink his eyes,
and she, the Saucy Duckfeather riding
and riding the magic branch and even,

it became obvious that she was
enjoying the ride: and Coyote Man
blew white ash through a knothole,
and what with her sweat and imagination

and secret longing, she just knew
she was turning white, and being
ridden four nights steady, Coyote
Man was content to leave and

left, and she, poor Saucy Duckfeather was
left with knowledge of her greed and
the acceptance of her given life
with her greyish, long-tailed children,

and old Magpie Woman stirred her
salmon soup and to the idle or curious
would only say, "well, that's the way
of doctors, especially if they're coyote."

Like the impetuous gluttony discussed in chapter 6, the gross
eroticism of Old Man Coyote is not so easy to relate to the be-
havior of *Canis latrans*. According to J. J. Kennelly (1978), the
female coyote—unlike her cousin, the domestic bitch—comes
into heat once a year and enters into a monogamous couple that
remains stable for at least the first year of the pups' lives. Ac-
cording to Ryden, "Coyote-watchers believe that in many cases

he pair bond in coyotes persists through life" (1975:67). Per-
haps, then, the lechery of Old Man Coyote reflects a projection
of human qualities onto the canid species. In any case, biological
similarities exist between the sexuality of coyotes and that of hu-
mans: protracted courtship and a degree of monogamy are
characteristic, at least sometimes, of both species (see Ryden
1975:68).

8 ▼ COYOTE THE THIEF

Although Coyote's thievery is frequently in the ultimate interest of the human race which is to come, it is clear that Coyote enjoys stealing for its own sake and for the joy of the trickery involved. In Karuk mythology, Coyote retrieves fire from "the upriver end of the world" by theft. Taking a relay team with him as he travels upriver, he finds a house at his destination in which only children are playing (Bright 1979:120–121). He lies down, pretending to rest.

▼▼▼
COYOTE STEALS FIRE

[Told in Karuk by JULIA STARRITT. Translated with WILLIAM BRIGHT.]

So then that's how they went upriver.
And Coyote arrived upriver.
And he saw it was empty.
And in the mountains he saw there were fires,
   there were forest fires,
      up in the mountain country.
And he went in a house.
And he saw only children were there.

And he said:
    "Where have they gone?
"Where have the men gone?"
And the children said:
    "They're hunting in the mountains."
And he said:
    "I'm lying down right here,
      I'm tired."
And he said to the children:
    "I'll paint your faces!
"Let me paint your faces.
"You'll look pretty that way."
And the children said:
    "Maybe he's Coyote."
They were saying that to each other.
And they said to him,
    to Coyote:
      "Maybe you're Coyote,
And he said: "No.
"I don't even know
    where that Coyote is.
"I don't hear,
    I don't know,
      the place where he is."
And he said:
    "Let me paint your faces!"
And when he painted all the children's faces,
    then he said:
      "See, I've set water down right here,
        so you can look into it.
"Your faces will look pretty!"
"But I'm lying down right here,
    I'm tired."

In fact, he had stuck fir bark into his toes.
And then he stuck his foot in the fire.
And then finally it caught fire well,
   it became a coal,
      it turned into a coal.
And then he jumped up again.
And he jumped out of the house.
And he ran back downriver.
And when he got tired,
   then he gave the fire to the next person.
And he too started running.
And in the mountain country,
   where there had been fires,
      then they all were extinguished.
And then people said,
   "Why, they've taken it back from us,
      our fire!"

Thus, fire is brought back to "the center of the world"—just in time for the creation of humans.

Sometimes Coyote's stealing is less successful. Leslie Silko (1981:239) tells how Toe'osh—Coyote, in the language of her Laguna Pueblo—tried to steal the food from a picnic being held at the bottom of a cliff. As often related in the Southwest, Coyote can occur as a multiple of himself.

▼▼▼
"WHAT STINKS?"

[Excerpt from "Toe'osh: A Laguna Coyote Story," by LESLIE SILKO, in *Storyteller*.]

They were after the picnic food
that the special dancers left

down below the cliff.
And *Toe'osh* and his cousins hung themselves
down over the cliff
holding each other's tail in their mouth making a coyote
  chain
until someone in the middle farted
and the guy behind him opened his
mouth to say "What stinks?" and they
all went tumbling down, like that.

Coyote is also known, of course, for stealing songs, stories,
and names. The Hopi/Miwok writer Wendy Rose sees him as
even stealing the poet's thoughts (1980:70–71).

▼▼▼
TRICKSTER

[From *Lost Copper*, by WENDY ROSE.]

Trickster's time
is not clicked off neatly
on round dials nor shadowed
in shifty digits;
he counts his changes slowly
and is not accurate.
He lives in his own mess of words,
his own burnt stew; he sees
when the singers are spread
and trapped by their songs,
numbed by the sounds of space
and reach their limit
so they can't hear the frozen music
circle above us like ravens or

like grubs flow into fleshy thrums
at their feet.

Trickster turns to wind,
Trickster turns to sand,
Trickster leaves you groping,
Trickster swings walking off
            with your singer's tongue
            left inaudible,
Trickster dashes under cars
            on the highway and leaves
            the crushed coyote,
Trickster bounces off whistling
            with his borrowed coat of patches
            and upside-down kachina mask,
Trickster licks stolen soup from his face
            and counts the slaps
            that hover in the silence
            near the place where
            they missed his face.
We see only his grey tail
bird-disguised
like a moving target
as he steals all the words
we ever thought
we knew.

From the viewpoint of *Canis latrans*, of course, "theft" is not
a relevant category—except in that coyotes, like other scaven-
gers, can be observed to sneak scraps of meat from kills made
by larger predators. If the coyote is a "thief," it is only by the
application of *human* moral standards.

Deception is of course the essence of Coyote's nature as a trickster, and it has been repeatedly illustrated here. I will only add a Diegueño story from Mexico, recorded by Leanne Hinton (1978), in an attempt at "ethnopoetic" re-translation by myself, which shows how Coyote remains himself even after conquest and hispanization.

▼▼▼
COYOTE BAPTIZES THE CHICKENS

[Told in Diegueño by ALEJANDRINA MURILLO MELENDRES. Translated by MARÍA ALDAMA and LEANNE HINTON. Adapted by WILLIAM BRIGHT.]

An old woman had a
hen and a rooster—
The hen had seven chicks . . .
Coyote came, he wanted to
carry them all off and
eat them, but he couldn't—

He saw the hen at the door,
he said, "Give me a chick, . . .
I'll take and baptize it," said Coyote—

"All right, take it"—
He took the chick and ate it—

The next day he came
and took still another one—
"Comadre, I'm taking another one to baptize,
the first one is sad, all by himself"—
He carried it off and ate it—
The baptizing was a fake!

The next day he came
and took still another one—
He carried them all off,
he ate up every chick.

Then he came: "Comadre,
come see your children, all baptized,
very big and beautiful;
they want to see you"—
"Go ahead," said the rooster—
Coyote carried off the hen,
he carried her off and ate her—

After eating he came back—
"Compadre, now Comadre cries for you to come . . ."
"All right," the rooster said, and went—
Coyote carried him off,
Coyote carried him off and ate him—

When he finished eating,
the old farmer's wife came—
"What happened to my chickens?
"They're lost, gone—what happened?
"Who robbed me?"

She went to look: Aah, a big cave;
under a stone were a lot of feathers—

All the chicks were eaten,
the hen and all, the rooster and all, all, were eaten—
the old woman went there and saw it,
she got furious: what could she do?
They were all gone.

It is not hard to see this story as an allegory of the historical
relationship between the Indians of Mexico and their hispan-
ized neighbors. It is worth noting that in the Southwest United
States and in Mexico the term *coyote* is used by many Indian
groups to refer to "half-breeds" or Spanish-speaking mestizos,
and that on the border between the United States and Mexico
coyote refers to the "migrant labor brokers" who guide undoc-
umented immigrants across the border—sometimes to their
death in the desert, if not into the arms of the U.S. immigration
authorities.

"Cheating" is, of course, like theft, a fairly irrelevant concept
from the viewpoint of the biological coyote; again, we can apply
such a term to coyote behavior only by the imposition of human
moral values.

It might seem redundant to characterize Coyote as an "outlaw" when he has already been convicted of so many crimes. But it is worth emphasizing the active *glee* that Coyote seems to take in flouting every social rule. He commits outrages that the First People have apparently not even thought of before, but in so doing he provides an *Erschreckensbeispiel*—a "horrible example" of how the human race should *not* behave, as when, in a Karuk myth, he eats his own excrement (Bright 1957:200).

In a Navajo myth told to Toelken by his consultant Yellowman, Coyote (Ma'i) attempts a double–double-cross when he persuades Skunk to help him catch some prairie dogs (Toelken and Scott 1981:97–103).

▼ ▼ ▼

COYOTE AND THE PRAIRIE DOGS

[Told in Navajo by YELLOWMAN. Translated with BARRE TOELKEN and TACHEENI SCOTT.]

Ma'i was trotting along [having always done so].

At a place I'm not familiar with called "Where the Wood Floats Out" he was walking along, it is said.

Then, also in an open area, it is said,
    he was walking along in the midst of many prairie dogs.

The prairie dogs were cursing him, it is said,
    all crowded together, yelling.

He went along further into their midst.

Then he walked further.

He got angry and soon began to feel hostile.

After a while it was noon.

He wanted [implied: looking upward] a cloud
    to appear
(His reason was that he started hating the prairie dogs),
    so he asked for rain.

Then a cloud appeared, it is said.
"If it would only rain on me," he said.
And that's what happened, it is said.

"If only there could be rain in my footprints."
And that's what happened, it is said.
"If only water would ooze up between my toes as I walk
    along," he said.

Then everything happened as he said, it is said.

"If only the water would come up to my knees," he said.
And that's what happened.

"If only the water would be up to my back
    so that only my ears would be out of the water."

"If I could only float," he said.
Then, starting to float,
"Where the prairie dogs are,
    if I could only land there," he said.

He came to rest in the midst of the prairie dog town, it is
    said.

Someplace in the *diz*—
    (*diz* is the name of a plant that grows in clumps)—
    he landed [implied: along with other debris] hung up
    in the clump, it is said.

And there he was lying after the rain.
And then Golizhi was running by to fetch water.
    (Ma'i was pretending to be dead)
Then he [Golizhi] was running.
He [Ma'i] called out to him, it is said.
"Come here," he said, and Golizhi came to him,
    it is said.

"Shiłna'ash," he said [very seriously].

"'The hated one has died, and has washed up
    where the prairie dogs are,' tell them that, shiłna'ash."

"'He's already got maggots,' you tell them," he said.

"Slendergrass, it is called—shake that Slendergrass
    so the seeds fall off.
In my crotch, in my nose, in the back part of my mouth,
    scatter some around, then put some inside my ears," he
    said.
"'He's got maggots,' you tell them.
'The hated one has been washed out.'"

"Make four clubs and put them under me.

'We'll dance over him.
We're all going to meet over there,'
    you tell them," he said.

"This is how," he said.
. . . . "dancing around" . . .
[implied: Golizhi is to join in these actions]
. . . " 'Hit Ma'i in the ribs' ". . . .

"Be careful not to hit me too hard!
'Slowly, gently, like this,'
     you tell them," he said.

This happened.
He ran home, and gave out the word to the prairie dogs, it
     is said.
"The hated one is washed out."

There were rabbits and other animals [there],
     and even groundsquirrels.
(Those animals which are food for him were gathered)
Now the people were dancing, it is said, at the meeting.

First, he [Golizhi] said, "It's true! It's true!
Let's have one of you who runs fast run over there to find
     out."

Then Jackrabbit ran and, "It's true!" said,
     running back, it is said.

Then Cottontail ran and, "It's true!" said,
     running back, it is said.

Then Prairie Dog ran and, they say, "It's true!" said,
     running back, it is said.

At that time there was a big gathering.
They were dancing, [implied: couples periodically stepping
     into circle] it is said.
Whatever they were singing, I don't know.

"The hated one is dead," they were saying;
 the club is beside him; they were hitting
 him in the ribs, it is said.

Then they continued with what they were doing,
 and more and more people came.
Then Golizhi-ye-ne said (remembering Ma'i's plan)
"You are all dancing;
While you are looking up, while you are saying,
 you say 'Dance in that manner,' you tell them
 while you're in charge there, shiłna'ash," he said.

Then they were dancing.
Then, "Waay, waay up there a *t'aadziłgai* is running through
 the air," he said,
 Golizhi said.

Then, when they were all looking up,
 he urinated upward
 so that it fell in their eyes, the urine.

His urine the animals were rubbing from their eyes.
" 'The one who is hated is dead?' " he [Ma'i] said, jumping
 up.

He grabbed the clubs from under him.

He used the clubs on them [all in a row, in one circular
 swing].
They were all clubbed to death.

Then,
"Let us cook by burying, shiłna'ash," he said.
"Dig right here," he said.
And he dug a trench, Golizhi did.

After he dug a ditch, he built a fire.
He put the food into the pit.
Then he [Ma'i] thought of something new.

"Let's have a foot race, shiłna'ash.
Whoever comes back first,
   this will be his," he said.
"No," he [Golizhi] said, but he [Ma'i] won the argument.
"I can't run fast," he [Golizhi] said.
"While I stay here, you start loping," he [Ma'i] said.

. . . while Ma'i pretended to do something
   to his ankles, he [Golizhi] started to run,
then, over the hill he ran,
   and ran into an abandoned hole.

In a little while, he [Ma'i] suddenly spurted away.

A torch he tied to his tail
and the smoke was pouring out behind him
   as he ran.

While he was running over there,
Golizhi ran back, it is said,
   there where he had buried the food.
He dug them up and took them up into the rocks,
   it is said.
Four little prairie dogs he reburied,
then he was sitting back up there, it is said.
Ma'i ran back, it is said,
   back to the place where the prairie dogs were buried.
He leaped over it.

"Hwah!" he said.

"Shiłna'ash—I wonder how far back he's plodding,
   Mr. His-Urine," he said.

Sighing, he lay down,
  pretended to lie down, in the shade.
He jumped up and leaped over to the pit.

He thrust a pointed object into the ground
  and grabbed the tail of the prairie dog first, it is said.
Only the tail came loose.

"Oh no! the fire has gotten to the tail," he said.

So he grabbed the stick and thrust it into the ground again;
  a little prairie dog he dug up, it is said.
"I'm not going to eat this [meat]," he said,
  and he flung it away toward the east.

He thrust it into the ground again;
  a little prairie dog he dug up.
"I'm not going to eat this," he said,
  and he flung it away toward the south.

He thrust it into the ground again;
  a little prairie dog he dug up.
"I'm not going to eat this," he said,
  and he flung it away toward the west.

He thrust it into the ground again;
  a little prairie dog he dug up.
"I'm not going to eat this," he said,
  and he flung it away toward the north.

He thrust repeatedly in many places, it is said,
  and couldn't find any.
Nothing, it is said.
There weren't any, it is said.

He couldn't, he walked [frustrated] around in circles.
He went around and he picked up those little prairie dogs
  he had thrown away.

Then he picked up every little bit
   and ate it all.

Then he started to follow [Golizhi's] tracks, it is said,
   but he couldn't pick up the trail.
He kept following the tracks, back and forth,
   to where the rock meets the sand.
(He didn't bother to look up.)

He [Golizhi] dropped a bone and he [Ma'i] looked up, it is
   said.
It dropped at his feet.

"Shiłna'ash, share with me again
[implied: what I shared with you previously]."

"Certainly not," he said to him, it is said.
He was begging, to no avail, it is said.
Golizhi kept dropping bones down to him.
He chewed the bones, it is said.

That's how it happened, it is said.

In an earlier discussion by Toelken of the same tale (1976:161–
162), he calls attention to "the high incidence of broken cus-
toms, or traditions ignored and transgressed." As he says,

Admission of hunger or tiredness is considered an extreme
weakness and is subject to laughter; begging help from
someone of lesser talents [as Coyote does from Skunk] is id-
iotic and subject to ridicule; begging for food is contempti-
ble and brings laughter; any kind of extreme, overinquisi-
tiveness, gluttony, and the like, is considered the sort of
weakness which must be cured by ceremony and is often in
the meantime subject to laughter . . . ; betrayal is
wrong. . . . In the tale above, one is struck by the presence
both of humor and of those cultural references against

which the morality of Coyote's actions may be judged. . . .
Causing children to laugh at an action because it is thought
to be weak, stupid, or excessive is to order their moral as-
sessment of it without recourse to open explanation or
didacticism.

But Toelken suggests that Coyote stories have a point even be-
yond their human and moral relevance:

The clown, then, . . . acts as a test, a challenge to order. . . .
Yellowman sees Coyote as an important entity in his reli-
gious views precisely because he is not ordered. [Coyote,]
unlike all others, experiences everything. . . . Coyote func-
tions in the oral literature as a symbol of that chaotic Every-
thing within which man's rituals have created an order for
survival. (1976:104)

In "neopoetic" terms, the actor/writer who uses the name Pe-
ter Coyote (1982:43–46) has described Old Man Coyote as
follows.

▼▼▼
MUDDY PRINTS ON MOHAIR

[By PETER COYOTE. Published in *Coyote's Journal*.]

Stand in a puddle of water long enough and even rubber
boots will leak. It is not surprising then, that after two cen-
turies of occupation, and despite conscientious efforts to
the contrary on the part of most humans, awareness of the
essential energies of this continent's plants and animals has
begun to exert an effect on transplanted Europeans,
Asians, and Africans; insinuating themselves into our
psyches and infiltrating our cultures.

Rings, charms, embroidered pillows, cruets, lorgnettes,

cookie jars, and clocks with eyes that move announce the supremacy of Owl as a totem for millions of Americans. Ceramic plates, statuary of varying dimensions, breast pins, drinking mugs, ashtrays and rings honor Frog. Each State has a native flower and bird associated with its sovereignty; sports teams compete under the heraldry of Bluejay, Hawk, Cougar, Bear and Lion. Consciousness of Whale, Baby Seal, pure water, clean air, sanctity of wilderness, snail darter, minute butterflies and salamanders has been the vehicle of massive political organizing. Even the Citizens Band Airwaves are flooded with names of "Tarweed," "Porcupine," "Meadowlark," and "Stink-bug."

Some prostitutes, poets, Zen students and several varieties of libertine have re-discovered the wit and utility of the Coyote-Trickster archetype. They have joined with those Native Americans who continue to recognize the beauty and worth of their ancient traditions, in creating a small but vital host who find value in this half-mental/half-mammal being.

I count myself among the number whose spinal telephone is being tapped by Coyote. Having spent some time thinking about him, being addressed by his name, raising some Coyote pups, talking to those who know him and his traditions well, and as eager as any to see him gain his recognition in our physical and cultural environment, I am delighted to see hosts of contemporary references to him cropping up in re-discovered myths, journals of ethnopoesy, union organizing literature and Roadrunner cartoons. I cannot help noticing, however, the singularity with which most of these references herd Coyote into a limited and already overfull pantheon of American iconoclastic personalities.

Coyote absorbs Chaplin, W. C. Fields, Bogart, Garbo, Dietrich, Mae West, Dillinger, Midler and Cagney as more dated symbols of allegiances to personal codes. His once extensive range of possibilities and adaptation is being reduced to the narrow spectrum of anti-sociability and personal excess. An example is Coyote's (recent) association with Zen eccentrics.

Although Zen training and traditions stress personal experience and understanding (thus the aptness of the lone, homeless wanderer as a symbol), the three treasures of Buddhism are Buddha, Dharma (the teachings), *and Sangha* (the community of like believers and practitioners). The transmission of Buddhism owes at least as much if not more to those who chose to operate *within* the non-personal, non-eccentric framework of tradition, as it does to those who have remained without. Personal liberation and tight community structure are not mutually exclusive, but in contemporary usage, Coyote is usually invoked as the crazy, enlightened loner whose purity is somehow measured by the number of forms and conventions he abuses. He is never (except in Native traditions) pictured as householder and community man. The rush to overlook this is a Coyote tricking that bears some watching.

I thought that it might serve our burgeoning interest in Coyote to share something of my own experience of his range of habitats, terrains, and markings so that future students not diminish his potential by maladaption, or make the too frequent error of designating wide varieties of adaptive possibilities within one species as hosts of sub-species. It is to this that I dedicate the following.

Coyote is the miss in your engine.
He steals your concentration in
the Zendo. Mates for life. A good
family man who helps raise the kids.

A good team player, but satisfied
to be alone. He's handsome and
well groomed: teeth, hair, and eyes
shine. He likes prosperity and goes
for it: a tough young banker bearing
down at a high stakes tennis game.

He is total effort. Any good after-
noon nap. Best dancer in the house.
The dealer and the sucker in a
sidewalk Monte game. An acquaintance
that hunts your power. The hooker
whose boyfriend comes out of the
closet while your pants are down.
He's also the boyfriend.

He eats grasshoppers and Cockerspaniels.
Drinks out of Bel-Aire swimming pools,
rainwater basins and cut lead-crystal
tumblers. He brings luck in gambling.
Inspires others to write about him. He
is jealousy.

A diligent mother. Top fashion model
with a fearless laugh. Easily bored.
He forgets what he was knowing.
He pretends to forget. Usually
gets the joke. Rarely follows advice.
Acts out our fantasies for us.

Is in the Bible as Onan's hand.
He's the gnawed squash in your garden.
The critical missing wrench from
your toolbox. He is the one who
returns with a harpooned acorn.

He may be Sirius, the dog star,
who, like Coyote, wanders and dies
awhile then comes back: companion
to Orion, the hunter, who like the
rest of us hunting enduring value and
knowledge, never forgets the brightest
star in our heavens.

The quintessentially outlaw nature of Coyote is expressed by Ramsey's reference to his "hostility to domesticity, maturity, good citizenship, modesty, and fidelity of any kind" (1983:27). This is in some ways quite the opposite to the nature of the biological coyote—which, as has been observed, is a faithful mate (at least during the one-year breeding cycle). Coyotes are also conscientious parents: Kleiman and Brady note that coyote parents care for their pups for at least the first nine months and that some coyote families remain intact much longer (1978:175). Once more, Old Man Coyote seems not to reflect any "wildness" in the wild coyote. Rather, it appears that human beings, perceiving such traits of coyotes as their wandering habits and their appetites, have projected other characteristics onto them—reflecting, above all, the rebellion of humans against their self-imposed domesticity.

We have seen how Old Man Coyote is responsible for bequeath-
ing to humankind not the Eden of original creation but the ac-
ual world we know. In the Karuk myth related in chapter 5,
Coyote ordains that men and women will have to work for a liv-
ing, "so they won't be lazy." Elsewhere, as we have seen, Coyote
s the inventor of death (Sapir 1910:77–93).

▼ ▼ ▼

SEX, FINGERS, AND DEATH

Told in Yana by SAM BATWI. Translated with EDWARD SAPIR.
Adapted by WILLIAM BRIGHT.]

[A team of three Creators—Cottontail, Lizard, and Gray
Squirrel—are in the process of ordaining life on earth. Cot-
tontail institutes sex distinctions as we know them. Lizard
decides that humans shall have hands with fingers, like his.
Coyote opposes their decisions and insists on inventing
death, but comes to regret it.]

Women used to go hunting deer,
    they'd come back empty-handed.
Men, who were then women,
    would pound acorns,
    make acorn bread,
    stay at home like women.

Again the "men" went hunting deer
   they couldn't kill any deer,
   those "men."
The "women" finished pounding acorns,
   when the sun was up in the east,
   the sun was on the hill.
Only one deer was killed,
   although there were thirty "men."
There were that many "men"
   and thirty "women."

The people had no fresh meat,
   no deer were killed by the "men."
"It's no good,
   what shall we do?"
   said the "women,"
"The 'men' haven't killed any deer."
[The Creators:] "Let's turn the 'women' into men!"
[The women:] "Yes!"

The "men" arrived home,
   they were angry,
   the "men" were beating their wives.
[The Creators:] "It's no good,
   let's turn the 'men' into women,
   and let's turn the 'women' into men."

At dawn the "men" went off,
   they went hunting deer.
In the east, Cottontail was building a fire on the ground.
Now the people came,
   the "men," hunting deer.
He sat there,
   he who had built the fire.
He took smooth, round stones,
   he put them in the fire.

They sat around the fire,
    the ones hunting deer.
That Cottontail was sitting there.
The "men" didn't notice the fireplace,
    they didn't notice the stones.
Suddenly they burst into pieces,
    the stones in the fireplace,
    they flew in all directions.
"Shhh!" they all said,
    those who had been "men,"
    their private parts were split.

[The Creators:] "Let's make the others into men!"
So it was done,
    and they became men.
Now those that had been "men,"
    they became women.
They stayed home pounding acorns,
    making acorn bread.
Now the others went hunting deer,
    now they killed many deer.

Cottontail got up,
    "Hehehe!" he said.
"Yes, now it's good,
    now they're killing deer.
"Look at them!
    It's good they're killing deer."
The women made acorn bread,
    the women pounded acorns.
Hehehe! The people didn't die,
    the people were very many.

Coyote said,
    "I don't like people to be so many.
"The women are very many,

the men are very many everywhere,
  the children are very many everywhere.
"The people don't die,
  they just get old.
"There's no poisoning by magic,
  there's nobody to cry in winter,"
  so he said.
None of the people understood death.
Cottontail understood it,
  Gray Squirrel understood it,
  Lizard understood it.
They were the only ones that understood.

Their hands were like this,
  round, all in one piece.
"Let's cut the hands with a knife!"
  the Creators said to everyone.
Nobody had fingers.
"I'll make fingers!"
  said Lizard.
—"Why should you make them?
"Our hands are good already,"
  said Coyote to Lizard.
—"How will we shoot arrows,
  when we go hunting deer,
  when we go hunting small game?"
  said Lizard.

Coyote was sitting there to the north.
The others were sitting there to the south,
  Cottontail, Lizard, and Gray Squirrel.
"Our hands are no good,"
  they said to Coyote.
"What will the women do,
  when they pound acorns?

"People have no fingers.
"They could take hold of the pestle,
    if they had fingers.
"Let's make fingers!"
    said Lizard to Coyote.
—"They'll use their elbows as pestles.
"They'll hold the mortar down with their legs,
    when they pound acorns,
    when they pound sunflower seeds,
    when they pound anything,"
    so said Coyote.
"Mh, mh, mh, mh,
    that's how they'll do,"
    so said Coyote.

"Hey!" said Lizard,
    "That's no good.
"Won't they get hurt here,
    if they use their elbows as pestles?"
—"It's no good,"
    said Cottontail.
"I'll make fingers,
    they'll be good.
"All the people will have them,
they will go hunting deer,
they will do well when they shoot,
    if they have fingers."
—"Why do you want to change things?"
    said Coyote.
"I don't approve of changing them.
"Fingers are no good,
    people won't do well like that."

The weather was good,
    the sun shone through.

Lizard went south downhill,
   a short distance south,
   all by himself.
He sat on the ground,
   he leaned against a rock.
He looked around on the ground,
   he saw bits of flint.
Lizard picked up some flint,
   he cut through his hands,
   making fingers,
   he cut both his hands.

Many people were living together.
Lizard was out of sight, south of a hill.
He looked back up to the north,
   he looked back at his hands,
   he moved his hands around like this.
"Hey, look at my fingers!"
They looked at Lizard's fingers.
"Hey, my fingers!"
People looked at them.
Lizard put them back down among the rocks,
   he didn't want people to see right away.
"Well! Hui!"
Women, children, men, all saw his hands.
Three times he did this,
   raising them quickly.
Three times he put them back down.
"Hui! He's fixed his hands,
   he's fixed them."
Coyote didn't see,
   he knew nothing about it.

[Lizard:] "That's how they'll do,
   look how they'll draw their bows!"

—"Fix mine also,
    cut my hands!"
    a person said.
Now he cut them,
    he made five fingers on people's hands.
"Look! now they'll kill deer,
    now they'll catch salmon.
"Women will do like this,
    now that they have fingers,
"when they pound anything,
    they'll hold the pestle in their hands.
Now we have good hands."
He came back uphill from the south,
    he'd cut everybody's hands.

Coyote saw it.
"What are you people doing to your hands?
"Mh! do it to me too,
    cut my hands,"
    he said to Lizard.
"No," said Lizard,
    let your hands be as they are."
Coyote said nothing.

Now people went hunting deer,
    killing deer with arrows, bows, flints,
    now that they had fingers.
Lizard said,
    "When women bear children,
    the babies will have fingers already."
Now he finished fixing their hands.
"Now they're good,
    our hands are good,"
    all the people said.
"Why should we say more about it?

Our hands are good now."
He didn't make fingers for Coyote.
Coyote was sitting on the north side of the sweathouse,
    he was hanging his head like this.

The people were very many,
    the people were like blackbirds.
There was no one who died,
    no poisoning by magic,
    no one who wept.
The men grew old,
    but didn't die.
The women grew old,
    but didn't die.

It rained.
All the people went in the sweathouse together.
Then it snowed.
Now Coyote had a child.
Coyote said,
    "Let's make people die!"
    speaking to the three [creators].
They were sitting there on the south side of the sweathouse.
Lizard had his head hung down.
Cottontail was sitting there,
    Gray Squirrel was sitting there,
All three had their heads hung down,
    listening to Coyote's words,
"It will be good if people die."

Now they spoke,
    Cottontail, Gray Squirrel, Lizard.
"Hm, hm, hm!" said Lizard,
"People shall not die,

so we won't weep when people die,"
said Lizard,
"In fact people will die,
    but they will come back to life.
"We'll bury them when they die,
    and they'll come back up.
"We won't bury them deep,
    when we bury them,
    when they die."
—"Why should they come back to life?"
said Coyote.
"When they die, they'll die.
"When people die,
    we'll weep,
    'Boo-hoo,' people will say.
"People will weep,
    when their brother dies,
    when their sister dies,
    when their child dies.
"Hoo! So they'll put pitch on their eyes,
    so they'll put clay on their faces,
    they'll mourn.
" 'Wai! wai! wai!' they'll say,
    when people weep."
What could Lizard say?
He was defeated.

Now it was snowing,
    the trees were all covered with snow.
They whispered together,
    Lizard, Gray Squirrel, Cottontail.
The people were afraid to go out in the snow,
    the people filled the sweathouse completely.

A man was sick,
   Lizard himself had poisoned him.
The sick man died.
Coyote said nothing.

A man was dead,
   but people did not weep.
"What shall we do with the dead man?"
   said Cottontail.
—"Let's bury him."
—"Where shall we bury him?
"There's too much snow outside.
"Let's bury him here in the sweathouse,
   in the floor on the south side."
Now they dug a pit,
   now they laid him in the pit,
   not very deep in the ground.
They covered him with earth,
   while the snow was still falling.

When he'd been buried,
   when he'd been laid in the pit,
he kept moving the gravestones around.
Coyote was sitting there like this,
   looking at the gravestones.
The dead man did like this,
   moving the gravestones around.
He was about to come back to life,
   he who had died,
   the dead man kept moving them around.
Coyote was looking at him,
   as he moved them around,
   he kept watching him.
The dead man came up this far from the grave.
Coyote jumped up,

Coyote jumped on the dead man,
   he pushed him down in the earth.
"Die!" said Coyote.
Coyote raised his foot,
   he did like this,
   he forced the dead man down with his foot.
"Why are you coming back to life?
"Die! Die!"
So he did,
   forcing him down with his foot.
The people said nothing against it.
Coyote left him and returned to his seat,
   he sat down again at the north side.
Again he looked at the gravestone,
   they weren't moving around any more.
Truly, the man was now dead for good.
"Now!" said Coyote,
   "Cry! weep!
"Now the man is dead,
   now we'll never see him again.
"Come on! Put on white clay for mourning!
   Come on! Smear your faces with pitch!"

Well, now the people finished.
"Come on, let's go hunting deer!"
   said the people.
Coyote's young son went along,
   hunting the deer.
"What shall we do to him?
   Let's make Coyote weep!"
   so said the people.
The trail ran east,
   a yellow pine stood not far to the east,
   the trail ran near the yellow pine.

"What shall we do?
    Let's make a rattlesnake!"
—"Yes!" said the people.
Now they made a rattlesnake in the east.
"Be coiled around the tree there!"
    they told the rattlesnake.
"Yes," it said.
They put it there where the yellow pine stood.

Now young Coyote came from the west on that trail.
Truly now there was a rattlesnake there,
    they had put it down for young Coyote.
Now young Coyote went up to the rattlesnake,
    suddenly it struck at young Coyote.
It curled around the coyote's legs,
    he was shouting,
    it was pulling him around and biting him.
The rattlesnake killed young Coyote,
    young Coyote died.

"Your child is dead,"
    so said all the people.
—"Where is he?"
—"He's dead in the east,
    he's been bitten by a rattlesnake."
Coyote said, "So!"
    now weeping,
    now dancing with grief.
Coyote was putting dirt on his face,
    acting like a crazy man.

People brought young Coyote back home.
Coyote said, "Friend,"
    talking to Lizard,
    dancing with grief.
"Wai! wai! wai!

"Friend, you said people should come back to life,
    after they die.
"Make my child come back to life.
"I don't like weeping so much.
"Make him come back to life!"

"Hm! hm!" said Cottontail.
"Cry, cry!
"You said people would cry.
"Weep, weep!
"Put white clay on your face,
    put pitch on your face!
"You said people would weep,
    if someone's brother died,
    so you said, you told me.
"Weep, weep!"

Among the Blackfeet of Montana and Alberta, the trans-
ormer figure is not called Coyote, but *Na'pi*, "Old Man"; the
imilarity of this name to that of Old Man Coyote can hardly be
coincidence. In the Blackfeet myth, Na'pi creates natural land-
narks, plants, and animals; then he creates human life, in the
orm of a woman and a child. The scene is set for the issue of
nortality. Like Coyote, Na'pi ordains the permanence of
leath—but with an additional motive, as explained by Ramsey
1983:8–10).

▼▼▼
FIRST WOMAN INVENTS COMPASSION

Excerpt from *Reading the Fire*, by JAROLD RAMSEY.]

Now at this point in the Blackfeet genesis, as so often in
these Western Indian accounts of creation, the first human
death occurs, and with it is broached, and significantly *lost*,

the possibility of a natural return to life after dying. Again, the emphasis in the narrative of these grave doings is not so much etiological, as imaginative and interpretive—a story is given that seems calculated to render death and its finality imaginable, even acceptable, according to our knowledge of human strengths and failings. And from a symbolic perspective, how wonderfully fitting—art, not accident, surely—that it should all commence as the first humans stand gazing, with Old Man, at a *river!*

As they were standing by the river, the woman said to him, "How is it? Will we always live, will there be no end to it?" He said, "I have never thought of that. We will have to decide it. I will take this buffalo chip and throw it in the river. If it floats, when people die, in four days they will become alive again; they will die for only four days. But if it sinks, there will be an end to them." He threw the chip into the river, and it floated. The woman turned and picked up a stone, and said, "No, I will throw this stone in the river; if it floats we will always live, if it sinks people must die, that they may always be sorry for each other." The woman threw the stone into the water, and it sank. "There," said Old Man, "you have chosen. There will be an end to them."

It was not many nights after this, that the woman's child died, and she cried a great deal for it. She said to Old Man, "Let us change this. The law that you first made, let that be a law." He said, "Not so. What is made law must be a law. We will undo nothing that we have done. People will have to die."

That is how we came to be people. It was he who made us.

To approach this mythic episode as a *Just So* story about the origin of death is to miss its subtlety and power altogether. The question "why do we have permanent death" is not really to be answered, except on a rather brutal causal basis, "Because the first woman foolishly and most regrettably opted for it." This is what happens, of course, but it is not what the story seems to say about the relationship of human nature, and life and death. Consider the details. The woman, gazing at the endless flow of the river, wonders if human life will be like that, and she appears to conclude that it must not be, to be properly "human"; it must instead be limited by death. And as she competes with Old Man in the throwing contest, in which the sinking of her lifeless stone is to be decisive, "in the nature of things," over the floating of Old Man's organic buffalo chip, she gives a most compelling reason for establishing death as a condition of life: "People must die," she says, "that they may always be sorry for each other." Is it not true in all cultures that the knowledge of our shared human mortality, our inevitably fatal weakness, is the basis of all ethics, all compassion, charity, solidarity of kind? First Woman resolutely throws her stone, which will sink beneath the river's surface even as each of us will ultimately sink from life—and in doing so she establishes precisely what Shakespeare's Macbeth guiltily calls "that great bond / Which keeps me pale" (3.2.49–50): the inviolable racial bond, that is, of humans bound to each other in their common mortality, and therefore capable of being "sorry for each other."

Now, it is a conventional feature of most Western myth-narratives on this theme that an actor (most commonly it is Coyote) theoretically opts for universal death, as here, the usual reason being that if there were to be no end to life, the world would soon become overcrowded. But what an imaginative difference between this straightforward and rather positivistic "ecological" sanctioning of mortality, and the Blackfeet First Woman's richly ambiguous *moral* postulation of death's value-to-come!

But her choice, however resonant of the future, is still

hypothetical, "expert beyond experience" so to speak; and what happens next is characteristic of the subtle and unsentimental wisdom of such narratives. Having deliberately set the precedent for death in order to establish a compelling if abstract moral principle for all time to come, First Woman (like her counterparts in most such stories) then in fact suffers the first death—that of her son—and immediately asks Old Man to revoke the mortal law she has just ordained! Perhaps there is a measure of justice to be seen in this turn of events, given what she has just done; but mostly, I think, there is a poignant revelation of First Woman as *one of us*, a fellow mortal: capable of noble proposals and all-too-human lapses; capable of theoretical certitude and experiential regret; susceptible to helpless grief and a familiar feckless wish that "the laws could be changed" when we are personally affected by them. Mortality has now come terribly into the world, but not without human significance, and First Woman is learning the condition of her mortality, and ours: death is not explained, per se (how could it be, really?), but rather the purpose of the myth is to effect an imaginative accommodation of the fact of death to the condition of living. The last lines of the story sum up its accommodative and consolatory power as a myth with memorable simplicity: "That is how we came to be people."

As Ricketts writes, "For the trickster, who has rejected all supernatural aid and has elected for freedom, there is no hope for immortality. Man must accept the fact of his mortal nature, and even choose it, as the trickster did, for the good of himself and the human race as a whole" (1965:349).

We have seen abundant evidence of how Coyote's tricks frequently backfire; he becomes *der zerspottete Spötter*. This is especially true in myths from the Southwest: In his attempts to trick Badger out of his wife, or to hoodwink Skunk out of his feast of roasted prairie dogs, it is Coyote who loses.

Coyote also frequently winds up a loser simply because of his own bad judgment and unrealistic optimism. In the Karuk narrative of "Coyote's Journey" (Bright 1980a:24–25), he sets out with high hopes on a quest for money.

▼ ▼ ▼
COYOTE STARTS UPRIVER

[Told in Karuk by NETTIE REUBEN. Translated with WILLIAM BRIGHT.]

A man lived there,
  he had many strings of shell-money,
    Coyote saw him there,
      he saw him measuring shell-money,
        that person there.
And then Coyote said,
  "Where do you find it,
    that money?"
And then that person said,
  "At Klamath Falls."

And then Coyote,
   he went home.
And then he thought,
   "I'll make some string!
"I have to go to Klamath Falls!
"I'll go get that money,
   I like it so much."
And he made a lot of it,
   that string.

So he tied it in a bundle,
   that string.
And then he thought,
   "Now I'll start out!"

And then he hurried upriver,
   the string in a pack,
      the little bits of string,
         what he was going to string it with,
         that money.
When he had packed it up,
   he carried it upriver,
      that string.

In a following episode, Coyote's disappointments begin. We have already learned that he never reaches Klamath Falls, but ultimately returns home after many adventures and misadventures (Bright 1980*a*:25).

▼▼▼

COYOTE CONTINUES UPRIVER

[Told in Karuk by JULIA STARRITT. Translated with WILLIAM BRIGHT.]

Finally he had gone far upriver.
And he looked upstream,
   a tree was standing there.

He saw ten raccoons were sitting there.
And he said, "Aha, good!
"I'll make new pants,
and a shirt for myself,
and a quiver,
and shoes for myself."
And he ripped them apart,
his clothes.
And he tore them to bits,
little bits.
And he threw them downslope.
And he stood naked.
And so then he said,
"Now I'll shoot one!"—
and he missed.
And the raccoon jumped away downslope.
And again he shot at one,
again it jumped down.
And he missed every one of them.
And he felt BAD.
And he crept away downslope.
And he collected them,
all his torn-up clothes.

Coyote mends his clothes with the string he has been carrying,
thereby acquiring his ragged, patchwork appearance—a char-
acteristic referred to in other myths and in the poem by Simon
Ortiz in chapter 4.

The biological evidence indeed refers to the fact that coy-
otes often have unsightly coats (Gier et al. 1978:39): "Sarcoptic
mange occurs with the [mange mite] burrowing into the epi-
dermal layer of the skin, resulting in lymph oozing through the
skin and intensive itch which causes much rubbing or biting of
the infected area." The Indian's view of Old Man Coyote reflects
such facts.

In many stories, Old Man Coyote is depicted as the friend, neighbor, or partner of Wolf, Fox, or Badger. (In fact, biologists recognize that coyotes and badgers often live in a symbiotic relationship; see Minta and Minta 1991.) These personages provide contrasts to Coyote's personality since they are uniformly sensible, level-headed, and temperate. Particularly in his attempts to imitate Badger, Coyote regularly ends up by making a fool of himself and coming to disaster, as in the following story (Boas 1901:79–89). Note that the badger, like its relative the skunk, has glands that produce a strong odor. In this story, Badger, who is Coyote's younger brother, uses his strong scent to asphyxiate his prey.

▼▼▼
COYOTE AND BADGER

[Told in Kathlamet Chinook by CHARLES CULTEE. Translated with FRANZ BOAS. Adapted by WILLIAM BRIGHT.]

There were Badger and Coyote,
   they were catching birds every day,
   Coyote would catch two,
   Badger would always catch many.

Then Coyote said,
   "What do you think?
   Shall we send word to Sturgeon?"
Badger said, "I think so."
Coyote tied cedar bark to his waist,
   and he stood in the water.
A canoe passed him,
   Coyote called it.
Coyote said,
   "Tell Sturgeon,
   he should come and see our younger brother."

Those people said,
  "We'll tell him."

Coyote stayed a long time,
  he stayed a long while.
He saw a canoe,
  he told his younger brother,
  "Ah, a canoe is coming,"
  he told his younger brother.
Sturgeon landed,
  Sturgeon came up,
  he stayed a while.
Badger was groaning,
  Badger said,
  "P'ayaa, p'ayaa!"
Coyote said,
  "He always says this to me,
  and I haul him,
  I carry him outdoors.
  Come, help me!
  We'll carry him out.
  Take hold of his legs!"
Sturgeon got up,
  he took hold of the feet,
  Coyote took the head.

Then they carried him out.
When his feet were outside,
  then Badger farted,
  Sturgeon fell dead.
Badger got up
  they slaughtered Sturgeon,
  his roe was white.

  [Coyote and Badger dine on Sturgeon for several days,
then get hungry again. They send in succession for Beaver,

Seal, and Porpoise; each in turn is tricked, poisoned, and slaughtered. Finally Sea Lion arrives.]

Then Sea Lion landed,
    he went up to the house,
    he tried to enter Coyote's house,
    he got stuck in the doorway.
They took out two wall planks.

Then he entered,
    that Sea Lion stayed a long time.
That Badger groaned.
Coyote said,
    "He says this to me,
    he makes me tired,
    I haul him,
    I carry him out.
    Help me!
    We'll carry him out."
Sea Lion stood up,
    they carried him out.
When his feet were out,
    then Badger farted,
    Sea Lion fell dead.
Badger got up,
    they slaughtered Sea Lion,
    their house was full of meat,
    their house was full of fat.
Coyote said,
    "So we will always do,
    whenever we get hungry."
They ate a long time,
    they finished it up.

Then they got hungry again.
Then it became known,
   "Look, Coyote and Badger are killing people!"
Coyote tried standing in the water,
   a canoe passed,
   he tried to send word,
   nobody spoke to him.
He tried standing in the water,
   he saw nothing,
   he gave up,
   he went to the house.
For two days he tried to send word,
   he gave up,
   he went to the house,
   he saw nothing at all.

Then they got hungry.
Coyote mended his arrows,
   they went to shoot birds.
They went in the morning,
   they came home in the evening.
Badger killed many,
   Coyote killed one duck.

   [Badger is killing game by farting at it. The same thing is
described for the two following days.]

Every day was like that.
One night Coyote thought,
   "Let's trade assholes!"
—"What do you think, younger brother?
   We'll trade assholes."
Badger said,
   "I like my asshole."
He said,

"I know my asshole,
you don't know it at all."

[Coyote continues to fail at hunting, and continues to
nag Badger to make a trade.]

Every night Coyote made Badger weary,
    he kept making his younger brother weary.
Then Badger said,
    "You make me weary,
    let's trade."

Then they traded assholes,
    Coyote woke up,
    he was happy.
He thought,
    "Now I've fooled you, Badger,
    now I'll kill lots of birds."
He got up early,
    quickly he got up.
"Poo," he farted.
He stood up,
    he went out.
He took quick steps,
    "Poo, poo, poo, poo."
He took slow steps,
    "Pu, pu, pu, pu."
When he took quick steps,
    he farted, "Poo."
When he took slow steps,
    he farted, "Poo, poo,"
    he farted slowly.

Then they went to hunt birds,
    in the evening they came home.

Coyote was unsuccessful,
    only Badger had caught many.
Coyote would try to creep near,
    he would step quickly,
    he would fart, "Poo, poo, poo."
The next day they went again,
    in the evening they came home.
Coyote was unsuccessful,
    he had caught nothing,
    only Badger had caught many.

Coyote thought,
    "I made a mistake,
    I'll give him back his asshole."
—"What do you think, younger brother?
    I will give you back this asshole of yours."
Badger didn't speak.
Coyote was trying to control his asshole,
    he would creep near,
    he would get close to those ducks.
They smelled him,
    they all escaped.

Again they came home,
    again Coyote told him,
"I'll give you back this asshole of yours."
—"You're making me weary,
    I gave it to you,
    and you're making me weary again."
He told Coyote,
    "You take yours off first."
Coyote took off Badger's asshole.
Badger next took off Coyote's asshole,
    he threw it in the water.

Coyote's asshole was thrown in the water,
   and Badger put on his own asshole.

Coyote's asshole was washed away,
   the creek was swift.
Coyote chased his asshole,
   and Badger went far away.
Coyote was chasing his asshole,
   he arrived somewhere,
   he slept.
He got up early,
   he reached a town.
"Well, did my asshole go past here?"
   he asked those people.
"Ah, yesterday," they said,
   "The boys were trying to hit it with spears."
Coyote went on,
   his asshole was calling, "P'ahehe, p'ahehe, p'a!"

[This happens in four more towns.]

Coyote went on,
   his asshole was saying, "P'ahahe, p'ahehe, p'a!"
He reached his asshole.

Then his asshole was small,
   all torn from being hit with spears.
He put his asshole on,
   at last it fit him.
"Badger will be your name,
   you who fooled me.
"Generations to come will only fear your farts,
   you will not catch birds."

Then Coyote went far off,
   he kept on going.

We have seen that the appeal of Coyote's adventures is frequently in their humor. In many of the examples cited our laughter is at Coyote's expense when his tricks backfire on him. But it should be remembered that we laugh not only *at* Coyote but also *with* him—his tricks, whether successful or not, are clearly designed in many cases both to secure some goal (as in the theft of fire) and for the sheer joy of prankishness.

In an Apache trickster tale narrated by Rudolph Kane, L. J. Evers tells how Ba'ts'oosee ("sly fox"), alias Coyote, tricks his cousin (Ba'dotłizhe ("grey fox") (Davenport and Evers n.d.).

▼▼▼
COYOTE TRICKS GREY FOX

[Excerpt from "Ba'ts'oosee: An Apache Trickster Cycle." Told in English by RUDOLPH KANE. Transcribed by KATHERINE DAVENPORT and LARRY EVERS.]

This is how it was told
a long time ago.
Ba'ts'oosee,
he was stealing from that white man's garden.
He steals at night.
Here he comes again at night.

There was tar in the shape of a man
at the gate,
where he comes in.
They put it there for him,
Ba'ts'oosee.
He came in again at night.
He said,
"Get out of my way."

He just went like this . . .
and he never got his hand back.

And this side too. . . .

"I can kick too. . . ."

He got stuck like a ball in it.
Ba'ts'oosee,
he got stuck.

He said, "I can bite too."
He just bit into it.

That's how he got caught.

They put a chain on him.
The white men did this to him.

This is a *le'gocho.*

He was still chained up,
still.
That's when they started boiling a lot of water.
The water got very hot.

The idea was to put him in there.
That's why he was chained up.
That's when the other fox came along,
Ba'dotɫizhe,
grey fox.

"Ba'dotlizhe" is what they call the one with the long
    white tail.
That's what they call
Ba'dotlizhe.

"My cousin,
let me tie you up right here.
I'm going to be eating with them soon.
They're going to do it pretty soon.
They're boiling water."

They were going to scald him in the water.

He tied the other one up,
and he ran off.
Now,
Ba'ts'oosee ran off.

Now,
a group of people came up.
They said,
"That's not him."
Some of them said,
"That's the same one."
Others said,
"He looks different."
They knew him.

So they shoved him in the boiling water.
Ba'dotlizhe,
they put him in.
Heee,
it all came off,
his fur.

The one who took off returned.
"Why did they do that to you, my cousin?"
that's what he said.

Ba'ts'oosee.
Keep on going.
They came to where there was water,
where water runs.
Ba'ts'oosee
and the other one,
the other one.

"My cousin,
there's *ba'dos* in there.
It's mine."

"It's bread.
It's bread that goes in the ashes.
It's Apache bread."
The *Ba'* calls it "Apache bread."
Ba'ts'oosee.

This down here is the reflection of the moon,
way down under.
That's why he tells his friend to drink all the water.
Ba'ts'oosee,
that's what he said.

They started drinking it.
Ba'ts'oosee
just had his mouth on the water.
The other one was really drinking it.
Heee,
his stomach was big.

The other one had his mouth on the water.
He pretended he was drinking it.
That's how he lies.

The other one was just like a ball.
He was full

from water.
It was like that.
That's how they told it,
true or not.
That's how it was a long time ago.

Coyote's clowning is sometimes accented by his appearing in
multiple form, as we have already seen in Leslie Silko's telling
1981:239), but with a single personality. (He is sometimes de-
cribed as having a family, and in some stories, Coyote's wife has
a separate identity, as when she is said to be Frog. Elsewhere, as
we've seen, she is called "Old Woman Coyote" or the like.)
   The Nez Perce, in Idaho, tell a story in which two coyotes in
act have an argument about their identity (Aoki 1979:17–19).

▼▼▼
TWO COYOTES

Told in Nez Perce by HARRY WHEELER. Translated with HARUO
AOKI. Adapted by WILLIAM BRIGHT.]

Two coyotes went up the river.
Then they came to a big bench.
And from there they saw,
    people were living down by the river.
And each friend said to the other,
    "Go ahead."
Then each said, "No, you go."
And each said, "No."
And for a long time they argued,
    they contested.
Then the first said,
    "So you go first,
    they'll see you,

and soon they'll say,
'That coyote's going on the trail.'"
The second: "I'm not a coyote."
The first: "But you're the same as me,
we're just alike,
and we're both coyotes."
The second: "No, I'm really Anutherwun,"
so they contested.

Then the second said,
"Now you go first."
Then there was a ridge,
people could see everything from below.
When the first started out,
now he went on,
he went over a small ridge,
then people below said to each other,
"That coyote's going upriver."
And people came out.
And they watched the coyote going.
Then his friend said, "See?
That's what they said about you,
you're a coyote."
And the first said,
"Then you come too,
they'll say the same about you,
you're a coyote."
The second: "All right, now I'll go."

And he too slowly started walking on the trail from there.
And people said, "Ah, yet another one,
that's another one."
Then the second came and said, "See?
I'm not a coyote,
I'm Anutherwun.

See? The people said I'm Anutherwun."
That's all.

This seems more like a simple joke than a myth: There are
no cosmological consequences, and the story is not even clearly
situated in the time of the First People. Moreover, the coyote
protagonists seem surprisingly shy, given our usual expecta-
tions. Yet the reluctance in admitting to be identified as a (mere)
coyote turns up elsewhere in the mythic literature. In the South-
ern Paiute story of how Coyote gives birth (chapter 5), he boasts
of being a medicine man, and in Karuk mythology he boasts,
'I'm really one of the First People!"—something which none
other of that race ever feels the need to assert. Bruce Bennett
1980) updates Coyote's image as joker in the following piece.
Significantly, Coyote remains unnamed in the text of the poem.

▼▼▼
COYOTE AND THE GYPSIES

From *Coyote Pays a Call*, by BRUCE BENNETT.]

A troop of gypsies
camped out of town.

Someone who saw them
raced with the news.

The town went wild—

boats hauled up;
back doors bolted;

children walloped;
shades drawn down.

Everyone braced.

Signs disappeared;
gardens were trampled;

phones went dead;
there were nails in the road . . .

"Goddam them gypsies!"
somebody hollered.

"Let's get 'em!"

Well, you guessed the rest.
Not a trace of gypsies.

Not a scrap
to show they'd been there.

So somebody asked
"Hey, who was it saw 'em?"

and nobody knew.

Ramsey speaks of Trickster figures in general as "irrepressi-
bly energetic." Again, he notes that Trickster as bricoleur has
"something distinctly less transcendent than a divine plan or te-
leology to guide him—namely, his own impressionable, way-
ward, *avid* mind"—his "sheer vitality" (1983:27, 41).

Zoological studies report something comparable when they
note, for example, that the coyote, unlike many mammals, is "ac-
tive both at night and during the day" (Lehner 1978:129). Per-
haps even more to the point are the numerous anecdotal re-
ports of playfulness, such as that from Leydet (1977:65): "[I]t is
difficult to escape the conclusion that coyotes *do* have a sense of
humor. How else to explain, for instance, the well-known pro-
pensity of experienced coyotes to dig up traps, turn them over,
and urinate or defecate on them?"

4 ▼ COYOTE THE PRAGMATIST

t has been noted that the mythic Coyote is often seen as re-
ponsible for the real world of "birth, copulation, and death"
hich he accepts both for himself and for the human species to
ome. Many myths end with the statement: "And Coyote said,
The people will do just like that too, like I did'" (see Bright
957:205).

Coyote's realistic or pragmatic stance and his lack of interest
n abstractions have attracted a number of modern Coyote
oets, such as Bennett (1980).

▼▼▼
:OYOTE'S METAPHYSICS

From *Coyote Pays a Call*, by BRUCE BENNETT.]

"He's bigger than me
and a whole lot smarter,"

Coyote remarked
speaking of God.

"Only thing is
He isn't around much

and it's gotta be someone
lookin' out for the chickens. . . ."

Peter Blue Cloud quotes Coyote in a similar vein (1978:65).

▼▼▼

FRYBREAD STORY

[From *Back Then Tomorrow*, by PETER BLUE CLOUD.]

Coyote was making frybread dough
when young Magpie stopped in
to offer his own recipe.

An extra handful of flour and
another dash of salt, he said,
would assure very fine results.

Coyote chased him away, shouting,
"I'm not making very fine results,
    you asshole,
I'm making frybread!"

Elsewhere, Blue Cloud reports additional statements of Coyote's philosophy (1982:133–134).

▼▼▼

COYOTE, COYOTE, PLEASE TELL ME

[From *Elderberry Flute Song*, by PETER BLUE CLOUD.]

What is a shaman?

A shaman I don't know
anything about.
I'm a doctor, myself.
When I use medicine,
it's between me,

my patient,
and the Creation.

Coyote, Coyote, please tell me
What is power?

It is said that power
is the ability to start
your chainsaw
with one pull.

Coyote, Coyote, please tell me
What is magic?

Magic is the first taste
of ripe strawberries, and
magic is a child dancing
in a summer's rain.

Coyote, Coyote, please tell me
Why is Creation?

Creation is because I
went to sleep last night
with a full stomach,
and when I woke up
this morning,
everything was here.

Coyote, Coyote, please tell me
Who you belong to?

According to the latest
survey, there are certain
persons who, in poetic
or scholarly guise,
have claimed me like
a conqueror's prize.

Let me just say
once and for all,
just to be done:
    Coyote,
he belongs to none.

Since Gary Snyder has been such an important writer in familiarizing the reading public not only with Coyote but also with the practices of Zen Buddhism, it is not surprising, as Peter Coyote writes, that "some prostitutes, poets, Zen students and several varieties of libertine have re-discovered the wit and utility of the Coyote-Trickster archetype" (1982:43–45). However, Snyder himself had earlier made the following point (1977:88–89; the full article is reprinted in chapter 16):

> [The] always-traveling, always lustful, breaker-of-limits side of the Trickster could destroy any human poet who got locked into it. . . . [quoting Will Staple (1977:36)]:
>
> > You're the same as Coyote
> > when you forget who you are
> > that's all he ever did!
>
> Which is why, in one of my own poems, I say, "Beasts have the Buddha-nature / All but / Coyote." The *Mu* / "No" of the shapeshifter sets us free.

As Snyder says (personal communication):

> This is a rather subtle point. The Buddha can be called a Trickster because he causes us to study, practice, anguish over a truth which is as plain as the nose on your face. That truth is realized by an act of letting go: of the self-image, preconceptions, opinions, concepts & theories that one is always nourishing. The hardest to let go is the idea of "Buddha-nature" and the idea of "having" or "accomplishing" realization, of "having potential" etc.—so that paradox-

ically the person who has cut loose the ties & pulled out the nails "has" no Buddha-nature. Or has "no" Buddha-nature. That's all Coyote ever did.

So it is not a case of having consciousness and choice that sets Buddha/Coyote apart; quite a many miles beyond that: having no special consciousness; no need to choose; the condition of resting in the fluid totality of things. Thus Dogen: "We study the self to forget the self. When you forget the self you become one with the 10,000 things."

The shapeshifter can keep shifting because he has no fixed ego-notion. I see a bulldozer, "RRRRRR!"; a chicken, "Cluck!"; a cloud, . . . float by . . . ; a paradoxical & knotty intellectual problem, you energetically get all knotted into it until it gets loose by itself.

So, as many Buddhist teachers have done, Coyote reminds us out the dangers of intellectualization. Thus the American n Master Robert Aitken presents us with Coyote as guru in ese excerpts from *Coyote Rōshi Goroku* (1982:47–48).

▼▼▼
OYOTE RŌSHI GOROKU

y ROBERT AITKEN. Published in *Coyote's Journal*.]

COYOTE AND CHAO-CHOU

Coyote showed a student the following kōan:

Chao-chou was strolling in the garden with his attendant. A rabbit ran across their path. The attendant asked, "Your Reverence has great goodness and wisdom—why should the rabbit run away from you?"
Chao-chou said, "Because I like to kill."

Coyote asked, "What was Chao-chou's meaning?"

The student said, "The attendant foolishly attributed a quality of awareness to the rabbit, so Chao-chou showed him his mistake by speaking of a quality he himself did not have."

Coyote pointed his finger at the student and said, "Bang."

ESSENTIAL NATURE

A student asked, "Can Essential Nature be destroyed?"

Coyote said, "Yes, it can."

The student asked, "How can Essential Nature be destroyed?"

Coyote said, "With an eraser."

THE JEWEL-NET OF INDRA

A student asked, "What is the Jewel-Net of Indra?"

Coyote drew the student toward him, and bumped heads with him.

The student said, "If I had known that, I wouldn't have asked."

LIVING BUDDHAS

Everybody knows how Coyote Rōshi loves to collect Buddhist images. Once a disciple of Rajneesh wrote to him, saying, "You are always looking for wooden Buddhas. You should come to India and meet a living Buddha."

Coyote mentioned this letter to his students, and remarked, "Living Buddhas are all over the place, but a good wooden Buddha is hard to find."

EMPTY

A student said, "I have found that there is no basis for emptiness," and he and Coyote burst into laughter.

It has been noted that the mythic Coyote is often referred to, directly or otherwise, as "Old Man."[1] However, considerations of chronological age seldom seem to be of importance in Coyote's adventures: He has a grown daughter, but in one Karuk myth he is certainly not too old to lust after her—or too feeble to carry his house on his back to a different location to disguise from the girl that her new "husband" is really her father (Bright 1957:202–205).

▼▼▼

COYOTE MARRIES HIS OWN DAUGHTER

[Told in Karuk by JULIA STARRITT. Translated with WILLIAM BRIGHT.]

Coyote was living there,
   he and his daughter lived,
   his wife had died.
And the girl got big,
   and she grew up pretty.
And the old man fell in love with his child.
And he thought,
   "Let me tell her,
   'You should get married!
A man lives there,

he lives far off there,
on the other side of the mountain.
But he's sort of old.'"
And he told his child,
"But you'll live well.
"You should get married,
you've gotten big.
"And I've gotten old,
nobody will take care of you,
I've gotten old."
And she said, "All right."

"But his house looks just like our house.
"Everything that's inside,
it looks just like what's inside here.
"And he looks just like me,
the man does.
"His ears are reddish too,
just like my ears look.
"You won't be homesick,
everything looks just like our things.
"Go on,
but go by the far way yonder,
don't travel this way right here,
on the short road,
you'll do badly.
"You can come back to see me sometime."

And so she left.
And when she arrived,
she saw that everything looked that way,
as it had looked outside their house,
it was true how her daddy said it looked.
And when the man came out,
he was just like her father.
And so she lived there.

Then the man said, "Go see your father again."
So she left.
And she traveled again,
     the way she had come there.
And when she got back,
     she saw the old man sitting.
And he was happy,
     when he saw his child.
And she said,
     "It's true,
     everything looks like our things here,
     in my husband's house."

Then she left again.
And she said,
     "I'm tired of going by the far way yonder."
And the old man said,
     "Just go there again!
"Something might happen to you.
"This side is a bad place."

So then he packed up his house,
and he got back first.

Then after a while she thought,
     "I think he's deceiving me.
"Everything looks like our things,
     and he looks just like my father.
"Now when I go back to visit,
     then I'll see if the house is there."

And so she left again.
And she said, "All right,
     let's go back together now."
And he said, "No,
     you go back alone."

And so she went again.
And after she'd gone,
    he packed up his house.
So then the woman turned back,
    she saw there was no house,
    nothing was there.
And so she chased him,
    she saw a person traveling there,
    he was carrying a house.
"I see it's my father!"
So then she grabbed him,
    and she just chopped him up.

And Coyote said,
    "The people will do just like that too,
    the way I did."

Indeed, Coyote is always the most lustful and energetic of the
First People. Why, then, is he called "Old Man"? As Gary Snyder
says, Coyote has "always been old," and this is "not the oldness
of history, but the oldness of 'once upon a time'—outside his-
tory; in Dream Time, which surrounds us" (1977:90; see chap-
ter 16).

Paul Radin's discussion of trickster myths, though never men-
tioning Coyote as such, notes that the protagonist is usually "de-
picted as a being who has always existed, and as an old man"
(1972:124–125). Ricketts proposes a specific explanation from
a viewpoint of cultural evolution: "The more strongly the tribe
has been influenced by an agricultural way of life, the less im-
portant is the place of the trickster-fixer. . . . This fact alone
would seem to indicate that he is an extremely archaic figure,
belonging to the culture of primitive hunters and gatherers"
(1965:328). In Ricketts's view, this would explain why Coyote is
both "trickster" and "fixer" in many areas, but much less of a
"fixer" among the corn-growing pueblos of the Southwest

United States—and even less so in Mexico, where corn-based agriculture seems to have originated.

Radin presents a picture of the trickster as originating in the most psychologically primitive strata of the human mind (1972:164). According to Carl Jung, who contributed a chapter to Radin's book, the trickster is "obviously . . . an archetypal psychic structure of extreme antiquity . . . a faithful copy of an absolutely undifferentiated human consciousness, corresponding to a psyche that has hardly left the animal level" (1972:200). Ricketts expresses skepticism about the specifically Jungian analysis, but agrees with Radin that the trickster "is the most ancient figure in [North American] Indian mythology," and indeed in all mythologies (1965:333). Whatever psychological explanations may be offered, it seems that studies in comparative myth provide some validation for Coyote's credentials as an "Old Man."

It may be significant that zoologists also regard *Canis latrans* as "old." As R. M. Nowak writes:

> The living coyote . . . is the most primitive member of its genus in North America. This is not to say that the species is in any way less intelligent or adaptable than the larger wolves . . . ; indeed the opposite may be true. By the term primitive is meant that . . . the species represents the ancestral, *less specialized* condition [emphasis added]. (1978:5)

Features of neural anatomy, skull, and teeth indicate that coyotes have not become as specialized in their adaptation as wolves; for example, they are more omnivorous (see Atkins 1978:21). To quote Nowak further:

> These various characters should not be considered handicaps, in the evolutionary sense. [The coyote's] smaller size, and ability to utilize small prey and vegetation more efficiently, may help the coyote survive periods of adverse con-

ditions under which the wolf would perish. Indeed, this process may be occurring today as the wolf progressively declines through competition with man, while the coyote continues to thrive and even expand its range.

Nowak also provides some interesting paleontological data: *Canis lepophagus*, a precursor of *Canis latrans*, is known from the "Blancan period" of the late Pliocene and early Pleistocene eras, some three to four million years ago (1978:6–7). The development to *Canis latrans* shows that "the braincase became more inflated, at the expense of the sagittal crest." He goes on to say that "it seems most likely that *Canis latrans* already had developed by the end of the Blancan, and thereafter did not undergo any great changes" (1978:9). The Rancholabrean period of 8,000 to 500,000 years ago—named after the famous Rancho La Brea tar pits in Los Angeles—shows abundant remains of *Canis latrans*, along with those of the now extinct camel, mammoth, sabertooth tiger, lion, and dire wolf (Nowak 1978:9–12). Coyote bones from the same period are reported from all over the western and midwestern United States, from Maryland and Florida, and in Mexico as far south as Oaxaca.

It is evident, then, that the coyote is indeed *old* in two biological senses: relatively nonspecialized anatomy and paleontological antiquity. It is not to be expected, of course, that North American Indians would have applied the name "Old Man Coyote" because they knew that *Canis latrans* had been a contemporary of the sabertooth. It seems plausible, however, that early Native Americans applied the name in recognition of the coyote's talents for adaptation and survival—precisely the qualities for which *Canis latrans* is labeled "primitive" in biological terms. Coyote has, in brief, been around a long time; he has seen everything and tried everything—and if he has not learned everything, he has surely learned that the key to survival is to *keep* trying.

16 ▼ COYOTE THE SURVIVOR

In various versions of Coyote's travels as told by the Karuk, he "drowns," but immediately afterwards he is seducing young girls (Bright 1957:173). At a later stage he apparently "drowns" again and is washed ashore at the mouth of the Klamath River (Bright 1957:164–67).

▼ ▼ ▼
COYOTE ON THE BEACH

[Told in Karuk by NETTIE REUBEN. Translated with WILLIAM BRIGHT.]

When they threw him back in the river,
　　then he floated ashore at Requa.
And he lay there on the shore.
And after a while the yellowjackets ate him.
And he lay there like that,
　　flies ate him too.
Soon the ants ate him too,
　　he lay there like that.
And there were just bones by now,
　　only his bones lay there.
And still he lay there like that.

And there was still meat there,
    in his testicles.
And the yellowjackets thought,
    "Let's eat this!"
And so they ate that meat there.
And when they bit it,
    then Coyote jumped up.
And he said, "Atutututututu!"
And he picked up a stick.
And he hit them.
So Coyote did that,
    he almost clubbed through them.
So that's why they all have small waists.

The vision of Coyote as survivor has attracted a number of contemporary poets. Thus Will Staple writes (1977:35) as follows.

▼▼▼
COYOTE

[From *Passes for Human*, by WILL STAPLE.]

Hard to enjoy
    a supper of rocks and sand
so coyote
does what his bones say to do
    "stay alive"

The survival of Coyote in his mythic adventures, in the continued storytelling traditions of Native Americans—and, since Snyder's "A Berry Feast" (1957), in a flourishing tradition of Anglo-American "coyote poetry"—has been given its definitive and by now classic statement by Snyder himself (1977:67–93).[1]

▼▼▼

THE INCREDIBLE SURVIVAL OF COYOTE

[From *The Old Ways*, by GARY SNYDER.]

Of all the uses of Native American lore in modern po-
etry, the presence of the Coyote figure, the continuing pres-
ence of Coyote, is the most striking. I could just as well say I
am talking about the interaction between myth and place,
sense of myth, sense of place, in our evolving modern po-
etry of the Far West. Western American poets are looking
back now at the history of the West, and how it is that they
are using as much Native American lore as they are draw-
ing on, say, the folklore of the cowboy or the mountain
men. Why is this?

When the early mountain men, explorers, and then pi-
oneers, cattle ranchers, moved into this Great Basin coun-
try a hundred and fifty years ago, they found, particularly
on the west side of the Rockies, peoples, Shoshonean and
others (Salishan peoples in Montana), that they regarded
with some contempt, as compared say with the Indians of
the plains, the Indians who put up a lot of fight and had a
more elaborate material culture. The Shoshonean people of
the Great Basin and the California Indians have received
the least respect and have been accorded a position at the
bottom of the scale in white regard for Indian cultures. The
California Indians were called "diggers." The early litera-
ture is really contemptuous of these people. Ignorance of
the California Indians is extraordinary. I find that very few
people are aware of the fact that the population of native
people in California was equal to native populations in all
the rest of North America north of the Rio Grande, and the
greatest density of North American Indian population
north of Mexico was in Napa County and Sonoma County,

California, just north of San Francisco Bay. The image of
California Indians as shiftless and as having no interesting
material culture persists although they had elaborate dance,
basketry, feather-working, ritual systems. That irony, then,
is that these people who were the least regarded have left
modern poetry with a very powerful heritage—Coyote.

The coyote survives where the wolf is almost extinct
throughout the West because, as I've been told, he took no
poison bait. Strychnine-laced cow carcasses that ranchers
put out for the wolf were what did the wolf in. The coyotes
learned very early not to take poisoned bait, and they still
flourish. In the same way, from the Rockies on westward,
from Mexico and north well into Canada, in all of these cul-
tures you find the trickster hero Coyote Man to be one of
the most prominent elements.

Stories about Coyote, Coyote Man as he's sometimes
called to distinguish him from coyote the animal, Coyote
the myth figure, who lived in myth time, dream time, and
lots of things happened then. Over on the other side of the
Cascades, he switches names and becomes Raven. In the
Great Lakes sometimes it's Hare, but out here it's Coyote
Man. Now, is there anybody here who doesn't know what a
Coyote tale is like? A Basin Coyote tale? In folklorist terms
he's a trickster, and the stories of the Far West are the most
trickster-like of all. He's always traveling, he's really stupid,
he's kind of bad, in fact he's really awful, he's outrageous.
Now he's done some good things too, he got fire for people.
The Mescaleros say he found where the fire was kept. It was
kept by a bunch of flies in a circle, and he couldn't get into
the circle, but he was able to stick his tail in there and get
his tail burning, and then off he scampered and managed
to start some forest fires with his tail, and that fire kept
running around the world, and people are still picking it
up here and there. So he's done some good things. He

taught people up on the Columbia River how to catch salmon. He taught people which were the edible plants.

But most of the time he's just into mischief. Like, it's Coyote's fault that there's death in the world. This from California, Maidu: Earthmaker made the world so that people wouldn't get old, wouldn't die. He made a lake so that if people began to feel as if they were getting old, they'd go get in this lake and get young again, and he made it so that every morning when you wake up you reach outside your lodge and there's a cooked bowl, cooked mind you, of hot steaming acorn mush to eat. Didn't have to work for food in those days. Nobody died, and there was always plenty of food, you just reached outside the door every morning and there's some nice hot acorn mush. But Coyote went around agitating the human beings saying, "Now, you folks, don't you think this is kind of a dull life, there ought to be something happening here, maybe you ought to die." And they'd say, "What's that, death?" And he'd say, "Well, you know, if you die, then you really have to take life seriously, you have to think about things more." And he kept agitating this way, and Earthmaker heard him agitating this way, and Earthmaker shook his head and he said, "Oh boy, things are going to go all wrong now." So Coyote kept agitating this death idea around, and pretty soon things started happening. They were having a foot race, and Coyote's son was running in the foot race. Coyote Man's son got out there, and by golly, he stepped on a rattlesnake and the rattlesnake bit him, and he fell over and lay on the ground, and everybody thought he was asleep for the longest time. Coyote kept shouting, "Wake up, come on now, run." Finally Earthmaker looked at him and said, "You know what happened? He's dead. You asked for it." And Coyote said, "Well, I changed my mind, I don't want people to die after

all, now let's have him come back to life." But Earthmaker
said, "It's too late now, it's too late now."

There are plenty of stories about Coyote Man and his
sheer foolishness. He's out walking along, and he watches
these beautiful little gold colored Cottonwood leaves float-
ing down to the ground, and they go this . . . this . . . this
. . . this . . . this, this, this, this, and he just watches those
for the longest time. Then he goes up and he asks those
leaves, "Now how do you do that? That's so pretty the way
you come down." And they say, "Well there's nothing to it,
you just get up in a tree, and then you fall off." So he
climbs up the Cottonwood tree and launches himself off,
but he doesn't go all pretty like that, he just goes bonk and
kills himself. But Coyote never dies, he gets killed plenty of
times, but he always comes back to life again, and then he
goes right on traveling.

When Coyote went to the world above this one, the only
way to get back was to come down a spider web, and the
spider told him, "Now, when you go down that spider web,
don't look down, and don't look back, just keep your eyes
closed until your feet hit the bottom, and then you'll be
okay." So he's going down this spider web, and he's gettin'
kind of restless, and he says, "Well, now, I'm just sure I'm
about to touch bottom now, any minute my foot's going to
touch bottom, I'm going to open my eyes." And he opens
his eyes, and naturally the spider web breaks, and he falls
and kills himself. So he lies there, and the carrion beetles
come and eat him, and some of his hair blows away and
pretty soon his ribs are coming out. About six months go by
and he really is looking messy, but he begins to wake up
and opens one eye and the other, and he can't find the
other eye, so he reaches out and sticks a pebble in his eye
socket, and then a blue jay comes along and puts a little

pine pitch on the pebble, and then he can see through that. And he sort of pulls himself back together and goes around and looks for a couple of his ribs that have kind of drifted down the hill, and pulls himself back together and says, "Well, now I'm going to keep on traveling."

He really gets into some awful mischief. There's a story we find all the way from the Okanogan country right down into the Apache country about how Coyote Man got interested in his oldest daughter. He just really wanted to have an affair with his oldest daughter, and he couldn't get over the idea so finally one day he told his family, "Well, I'm going to die now," or in some versions he says, "I'm going on a long trip." So he just goes around the corner on the hill a ways, and he puts on a disguise. Oh, before he goes he tells them, "If a man comes along, some handsome man with a big satchel who has a couple of jack rabbits to offer you, now you be real nice to him, let him in, take good care of him." So then he goes off around the corner, puts on his disguise, picks up a couple of jack rabbits, and comes back, and the girls say to their mother, "Why, sure enough, here's a man just like Daddy said we should be nice to." And so they take him into the house, and feed him and he sits in the corner and talks in kind of a muffled voice, and then he starts saying, "That sure is a pretty oldest daughter you've got there, wouldn't you like to marry her to somebody? And he's almost going to get away with this, but then he asks them to go over his hair for lice or something like that, and so they're going over his hair for lice, and they find this wart on one cheek, and they say, "Why, it's just Daddy." Lots of stories like that.

How did this literature come down to modern American poetry? I was hitchhiking in 1951 from San Francisco to Indiana University where I was going to enter graduate school in anthropology. I got picked up by some Paiute

men just outside of Reno in the evening. We drove all night
to Elko. During that night it turned out they had a couple
of cases of beer in the car, so we were doing that old far
western thing of driving and drinking a couple of hundred
miles, and they started telling Coyote tales. They had been
working as steelworkers in Oakland, and they were heading
back home somewhere near Elko, and they started telling
Coyote tales. They started talking about Jesus, one said Je-
sus was a great gambler. He was perhaps the best gambler
in the United States. And they told Coyote stories with ob-
vious relish, as part of their own world, but also with that
distance of having been urban, having worked on steelwork-
ing jobs, having been to BIA school. Still telling them. An-
other way we come on it is this. In my own poetry, back 20
years or so, the Coyote trickster theme began to crop up
here and there. (I think I was one of the first to find some-
thing to use in that Coyote image, but I'm not the only one.
There's been a magazine called *Coyote's Journal* that has had
ten issues out now in the last seven years, edited by James
Koller, who first lived in the state of Washington, then lived
in the Bay Area and now lives in Maine, and the latest issue
of *Coyote's Journal* was produced in Maine.)

Jaime de Angulo brought together a book that had origi-
nally started out as stories he told to his children, first pub-
lished in the middle fifties as *Indian Tales*. (Jaime de An-
gulo was originally a Spanish M.D. who converted over to
being an anthropologist and linguist first in the Southwest
and then in California during the twenties and thirties, and
then became a San Francisco and Big Sur post–World War
II anarchist-bohemian culture hero. Now, he was one of the
people who had direct contact with Coyote and other
American Indian lore as a linguist and anthropologist.
Jaime de Angulo was a friend of Robinson Jeffers, in fact I
have heard it said that he was the only human being that

Robinson Jeffers would let into his house any time of the day or night. He appears in some of Robinson Jeffers' poems as the Spanish cowboy, because at one time Jaime de Angulo was running a working ranch on Partington Ridge up above Big Sur.) So Jaime de Angulo's *Indian Tales*, which is full of California Indian Coyote lore, is filtered through Jaime's own peculiar way of seeing things, and this became a direct influence on a lot of writers in the Bay Area. So there is a peculiar Western and particularly West Coast body of poetry which at one point or another refers to Coyote almost as though everybody knew what Coyote is all about already, and in some areas of the literary Western world Coyote is already taken for granted as a shorthand name for a particular figure which is out of the Native American Indian lore but also, in psychological terms, refers to something in ourselves which is creative, unpredictable, contradictory: trickster human nature.

I'd better step back and talk about the West again. I've noticed that all the experts here dodge off the question when anybody asks them, "What is a Westerner, really, what is the West?" Nobody wants to say. So I'll offer my interpretation of that, hoping that I have proper credentials at least by being from an old Western family, who did what I would consider Western things, used Western speech, and had a certain kind of Western set of attitudes. A certain set, there are several sets. The usual literature of the West is concerned with the period of exploitation and expansion west of the tree line. This is what we mean when we talk about the "epic" or "heroic" period of the West. A period of rapid expansion, first-phase exploitation. It is not a literature of place. It's a history and a literature of feats of strength, and of human events; of specifically white, English-speaking-American human events. It's only about this place by accident. The place only comes into it as a matter of inhospitable and unfamiliar terrain; Anglos from temperate climates suddenly confronted with vast, treeless, arid spaces. Space and aridity; confronting that and living with it is a key theme in Western literature, but only incidentally. It could just as well be an Icelandic saga or a heroic epic of Indo-European people spreading with their cattle and wagons into any other unfamiliar and new territory as they did in 1500 B.C. when they moved down into the Ganges River Basin or into Greece. The West, then, presented us with an image of manliness, of vigor, of courage, of humor, of heroics which became a very strong part of our national self-image; perhaps the strongest part, the most pervasive, the one which has been most exported to the rest of the world. There are, of course, Southern images: the Daniel Boone image; there is the Yankee self-image and several others in American folk literature/folk lore history. But the Western image, which is a kind of amalgam of mountain man, cowboy, and rancher, is one of the strongest self-images of America. The West ceases to be (whether it's geographically Western or not) when an economy shifts from direct, rapid exploitation to a stabilized agricultural recycling base. Heroics go with first-phase exploitation, hence fur trade, then cattle industry, then mining, then logging.

I grew up in an area where logging was going on. That's what made it the West, actually it was western Washington, which some people perhaps would exclude from the "Western literature" spheres since not arid and treeless, but it is within the West because it was within that sphere of direct exploitation which had the tall tales, the energy, the unpredictability, the mobility, and the uprootedness of that kind of work. The dairy farmers of the Willamette Valley of Oregon are not so much Westerners, they're New Englanders or they're Wisconsin People, they are in a different place. San Francisco was the jumping off point for the mines in

Nevada—that's again the direct exploitation, the rapid growth. Which is why the oil fields are Western, they still have that rough and tumble angle to them, and why the North slope of Alaska is the West in the senses of which I'm talking. (And we can expect, or could have expected a few decades back, that the oil fields of Alaska would produce some tall tale–type lore of oil-men.)

Another aspect: men removed some distance from women. Leslie Fiedler has talked about this in a very interesting way: saying that one aspect of the heroic and epic West is that men have gotten away from home and away from women. You may all know the movie in which finally the Bible totin' ladies come to town, and the men have to get all shiny and spruced up and there they are sitting in this little white New England–style church singing hymns finally, and it's funny and it's also tragic, you know. The West is over when nice women come and start making you wash your hands before dinner. Something Fiedler didn't say is that it's also men removed from the father image. They're beyond the reach of the law, which is to say the Nation State patriarchal figure archetype. And so the West is in a sense psychologically occupied by boys without fathers and mothers, who are really free to get away with things for a while, and that's why there is so much humor in the lore of the West.

But something has happened, since World War II. I can see a little bit how it happened in myself. Our sense of the West is changing from a history of exploitation and westward expansion by white people, into a sense of place. Those old time Westerners did not know where they were. Except for the mountain men, who became almost Indians, they didn't really know the plants, they didn't really know animal behavior. The mountain men were the quickest and the first to learn that. The process of learning "where they were"—of becoming natives of the place—was underway, I know how my grandmother was able to pick wild plants in Kitsap County, Washington, how she was able to use things from the forest, making berry pies out of wild blackberries, she knew a few edible mushrooms. But my grandmother's generation was the last of it; the next generation grew up with supermarkets and canned food. The potentiality of a viable self-sufficient rural West evaporated after about one generation. What we have now in the West is really an urban population, small town and urban people who are all driving hundreds of miles, operating with fossil fuels, and getting their food from supermarkets (with a few outstanding exceptions). Comparisons can be made, of course, with people of the hills of the South, or of New England, who had a hundred and fifty to three hundred years of living in a self-sufficient rural manner, and who really did develop a much deeper knowledge and self-sufficiency related to the plants, animals, weather patterns, the lore of the place. There *is* a sense of place in the South and in New England, although it has eroded considerably. But the Far West didn't really quite get it. So that when some of my colleagues, poets, for example, talk about, "Let's make an anthology of Western Poetry" or "Who is a Western poet? What is Western poetry?" the first criterion should be sense of place, and how well that comes across. Poets who have lived in the West all their lives, teaching in universities, can speak only of the urban world, some of them, and they're not paisanos, you see, paisanos in the sense of knowing a place. So there is a work to be done in the matter of knowing where we are, the old American quest, which I share with all of you, for an identity, a sense of place. To know the place well means, first and foremost, I think, to know plants, and it means developing a sensitivity, an openness, an awareness of all kinds of weather patterns and patterns in nature.

So, why do modern writers and some young people today look to Native American lore? Well, the first answer, there is something to be learned from the Native American people about where we are. It can't be learned from anybody else. We have a Western white history of a hundred and fifty years; but the Native American history (the datings are always being pushed back) was first ten thousand years, then it was sixteen thousand years, then people started talking about thirty-five thousand years, and now, with the Santa Barbara skull, fifty thousand years. So, when we look at a little bit of American Indian folklore, myth, read a tale, we're catching just the tip of an iceberg of forty or fifty thousand years of human experience, on this continent, in this place. It takes a great effort of imagination to enter into that, to draw from it, but there is something powerfully there.

There is a remarkable body of Native American myth and lore which resides in our libraries in the form of the bulletins and reports of the Bureau of American Ethnology going back to the 1880s. Respectable, scrupulous, careful collections, for the most part unbowdlerized. (In the early days they took the more scatological sections and translated them into Latin, but then everybody knew Latin in those days so. . . . But in recent years they don't do that.) That is what I learned from, there is an irony in that too. I grew up knowing Indians and not too far from them, but the first way I got my hands on the material was going into the library. Franz Boas, Edward Sapir, John Swanton, Melville Jacobs, Thelma Jacobson, Alfred Lewis Kroeber and his students and disciples, Harry Hoijer, M. E. Opler, almost all of them in one way or another disciples of Franz Boas, gave

decades of their lives to the collection of texts in the original
languages, and translations into English, of the lore of
every cultural group that they could make contact with
from British Columbia south. It is an extremely rich body
of scholarship and some of us learned how to draw it into
our own work, to enjoy it, first and foremost to enjoy it.
The first thing that excited me about Coyote tales was the
delightful, Dadaistic energy, leaping somehow into a mod-
ern frame of reference. The technical and scholarly collec-
tions of American Indian material have begun to creep into
more popular availability and circulation. Jerome Rothen-
berg's book *Shaking the Pumpkin* [1972], which is an anthol-
ogy of American Indian poetry, is the best to be done so
far, but I'm still dubious about what happens when modern
white men start changing the old texts, making versions,
editing, cleaning it up—not cleaning it up so much as just
changing it around a little bit. There's nothing for me as
useful as the direct transcription, as literally close as possi-
ble to the original text in whatever language it was, Kwaki-
utl or Apache. The true flavor seems to be there. (There is
a perennial argument, do you get more out of something
when somebody has made it more readable, more literary,
taken the brackets and the parentheses out, and the dots
and the ellipses and the footnotes, cleaned it up so you can
read it? Is that better or is it better when you get down to
the primary source and try to use that? Well, I'm all for the
primary source in historical materials, whether American
Indian or otherwise, because I would prefer to do the edit-
ing with my imagination rather than let somebody else's
imagination do the work for me. At least, then, if there are
errors in interpretation they're my own errors, and not
somebody else's.) That's just a footnote on the side, and to
point out that when these poets—such as Will Staple, Barry
Gifford, Ed Dorn, Enrique LaMadrid, Margo St. James,

James White, or James Koller use Coyote material, usually some percentage of their inspiration started at the library. Peter Blue Cloud may be the only exception.

The other twenty percent is not to be overlooked, though. The other twenty percent comes from that direct experience of being in the space of the West. How does it feel to be out in the deserts of Eastern Oregon, or Eastern Washington? I spent a lot of time in eastern Oregon, and going into it. Sure, stories about the early stages and wagon trains going across eastern Oregon, tales of the early wheat ranchers, they're interesting, but they don't help with the place. To tune to the smell of it, and the feel of it I found that the sense of Coyote and some of the other materials that, say, Sapir collected, Wasco and Wishram texts, began to teach me something about the real flavor of the land, began to move me back just a trifle from historical time into myth time, into the eternal now of geological time for which our historical time, one hundred and fifty years, is an inconsequential ripple. Those flavors. . . . Looking forward, then, I can only speculate that (just to finish with comments on ideas of the West) future Western young people, whether in Utah, Idaho, Nevada, California, or whatever, are bound to become increasingly concerned with *place*. This will not be the same as regionalism. Regionalism, as it has existed in American literature in the past has been pretty much a human history; the story of particular human habits, and oddities and quirks, and ethnic diversities and whatever, that are established in a region. That's white human history, often very good literature, but "regional" has not been so specifically tuned to the spirit of place as I think it will in the future. That exploitative first phase economic and social behavior, although heroic and interesting, is not a viable long range model. Ecologists and economists are beginning to tell us now that harmony with the local

place and a way of life that does not exhaust the resources
and can be passed on to your children and grandchildren
with no fear of depletion is the way we must learn to live.
As people come to understand this, they will look back with
few regrets, and say that the heroic period of the West was
entertaining, but we're learning a lot from the Indians.
And for the Indian peoples, Western history is not a glo-
rious epic history with nice tall tales on the side, it's a his-
tory of humiliation, defeat and dispossession.

Now, then, what of the trickster, himself? Coyote, as I
said, was interesting to me and some of my colleagues be-
cause he spoke to us of place, because he clearly belonged
to the place and became almost like a guardian, a protector
spirit. The other part of it has to come out of something in-
side of us. The fascination with the trickster. A world folk
image of the trickster, suppressed or altered in some cul-
tures; more clearly developed in others. For me I think the
most interesting psychological thing about the trickster, and
what drew me to it for my own personal reasons was that
there wasn't a clear dualism of good and evil established
there, that he clearly manifested benevolence, compassion,
help, to human beings, sometimes, and had a certain dig-
nity; and on other occasions he was the silliest utmost fool;
the overriding picture is old Coyote Man, he's just always
traveling along, doing the best he can. Growing up in the
fifties in Portland, Oregon; going to Reed College, associ-
ated with still struggling ex–Communist Party professors,
who had found the last haven, you know, somewhere to
teach. Drawing on IWW lore of my grandfather, native
white grass-roots political radicalism of the Northwest. The
trickster presents himself to us as an anti-hero. The West
was heroics, but as you know, in the fifties and sixties we
didn't feel like heroics, we felt more like anti-heroics, and
the trickster is immediately an attractive figure for the same

reasons that you find anti-heroics in the writings of post–World War II French and Italian or English writers. Artaud is a trickster, William Burroughs in his novels talks out of the side of his mouth with a kind of half Coyote, half Dashiell Hammett dry style. So the trickster image is basic; it has to do in part with that turning away from heroes. It's also interesting that there is a white American frontier language and story-telling which is often very much like Coyote lore—irresponsible, humorous, and unpredictable. Mike Fink stories and tall tales were being made up while these people were fighting with each other, the Indians telling their Coyote tales and the white men telling their tall tales, and they probably had very much the same sense of humor in some respects, but they weren't communicating across that gap. (I'm only reading Coyote as I can, namely twentieth century, West Coast white American. How the Native American people themselves actually saw Coyote, actually used it, is another question which I may be able to touch on in a few minutes.)

So, when the Coyote figure comes into modern American poetry it is not just for a sense of place. It is also a play on the worldwide myth, tale, and motif storehouse. Poetry has always done this—drawing out, re-creating, subtly altering for each time and place the fundamental images.

II

A poem by Peter Blue Cloud:

CAMP

by starlight hush of wind the owl's shadow voice,
the campfire embers glowing inner universe,
by firelight smoke curls weaving faint the voices,
coyote voices faint the pain and smell of pitch,

fire, I sing you stars,
fire, I breathe obsidian
& again the owl's shadow voice leans back.
into times past
      singing first fire,

brittle spine bent bowed toward the fire,

voices low to murmur a child whimper,
deer fat sucked upon to gentle dreaming
the mother her song the night cradles,
            child, the owl, too, has young,
            tiny hearts and warmth of down,
& old man coughing guttural spit to fire,
young people giggle beneath hide fondlings
            soon to sleep,
again coyote voices drown the mind in a loneliness
of deep respect in love of those who camp
            just up the hill,
& tiny crystals of tears spatter the dust,
            my people,
legs that cannot ever carry me back to you,
            soul that holds you
            forever.

The night, howl, gate to coyote-the-animal. Gate to the
People, and to the stories that lead on from there. Coyote
the animal is a perfect expression of a specific set of natural
relationships; as appropriate to the mountains and deserts
of the West as the Trickster image is appropriate to certain
human needs. It's a marvelous coming-together—the meet-
ing of Trickster and coyote. Coyote is smart, quick, omnivo-
rous, careful, playful; a good parent; opportunistic, and
graceful. People who know nature by direct observation
have seen all this; the Native Americans knew even more.

There are specific things to be learned from each bird, plant and animal—a natural system is a total education— and this learning is moral as well as being useful for survival. "The Redtail teaches us to have a broad view of things, while not missing the stirring of a single mouse."

And into the story: the oldest, funniest Coyote Man is in the long poems of Peter Blue Cloud. This is from "Snout"—

       . . . "bring Coyote Man and
we can all chase our tails." and soon, dancing sideways
and foot-shuffling, Coyote Man was the
               center of
attention as he stooped over to examine the ground
and soon a crowd was stooped over the same spot

as Coyote Man suddenly straightened up and,
"Hah! I knew it!" and studied the ground
some more, "yes, it was right here before, but now
it's gone, as you can all see," and ignoring any

questions, turned to Roundhouse-builder, "oh, I know
all about your son Snout and his sharp corners
don't forget that even a great doctor like
myself sleeps nose to ass in circle," and he

gave Bullhead Woman a friendly pat on her butt,
and whispered to that old and ugly creature, "It's
just because of you that I come down here, and tonight
you and me's gonna wrastle 'til sun-up, and she

giggled with pleasure, ignoring the knowledge of her
young daughters and nieces. And Coyote Man ate
and slept and dreamed and planned and walked about
muttering in his sacred manner, and made his

plans to cure Snout of his sharp corners and
nosey delvings into other people's lives, and
chose Bullhead's daughter Trout Girl for his
helper, and instructed her, mostly at night . . .

Yet the always-traveling, always lustful, breaker-of-limits
side of the Trickster could destroy any human poet who got
locked into it. The Trickster is a delightful literary conceit,
but an unpredictable Ally—dangerous and very potent. For
those who can handle such a Helper the power of being a
Healer may be gained.

Will Staple:

You're the same as Coyote
when you forget who you are
that's all he ever did!

Which is why, in one of my poems, I say "Beasts have the
Buddha-nature / All but / Coyote." The *Mu* / "No" of the
shapeshifter sets us free.

And yet, in the giving up/hanging on, there's another
price that's paid; Will Staple again:

yes, I am an old coyote
not yet well into my useless years.
o, i fool them, wearing clothes
standing upright, talking like a man.
i look over behind me and move pretty fast
                for an old timer
                        no longer a coy pup

not that i've changed my ways
the mind is on fire
red-eyed, burning.

whatever i had got me this far
this is what's left of what there was . . .
         a survivor.

Coyote Old Man. Not that he's "old" now, in white-man
times, but that he's always been old. Not the oldness of his-
tory, but the oldness of "once upon a time"—outside his-
tory; in Dream Time, which surrounds us. And out of
"Dream Time" comes the healing:

Hey coyote. Welcome
back to the cartoon.

Thank you my fran. Excuse me boy,
you got a cigarette?

Here, have a camel.
Whaddya think's goin on?

All my frans are doing fine.

What do you think are the trends?
Do you think people are living a little more natural?

What do you mean natural?
Like when you're living in a car
is that natural?

Right, but—

You must got to remember,
Illumination.
You got to give off some illumination
or the rest of us be thinkin
that the humans want it all for themselves.
And you pay for that in the long run, don't
you see.

I see.

Say. You know I don't have any money.

Oh. Well. I can go down to the liquor store
and cash a five. I have to go downtown anyway.

Heh-heh. No, that's alright man. Coyote's don't
use money. We usually naked. Don't have no pockets.

Coyote, are you a Buddhist?

I'm a *friend* of the Buddhist.

Coyote, what about marriage?

Boy, I'm afraid you're barking up the wrong tree.

It's just the same in your philosophy?

Boy, I don't have no philosophy.

Well how do you treat women?

I treat everybody good.
You have to,
if you're gonna live in a family,
which I'm hopin you're gonna *do*
because it's your ass if you *don't*.
Either way,
I'm gonna be a survivor.
If you know what I mean.

Lewis MacAdams, "Callin Coyote Home"

III

The Trickster is probably the most archaic and widely
diffused figure in world folklore. No wonder his name, sim-
ply, often, is "Old Man." He is the Old One, the Ancient
Buddha. It's hardly even worth it to ask what the Trickster

meant to Upper Paleolithic hunters; with a laugh and a shiver we each intuitively know—and can guess at the human mind-world projected from the most archaic constellation of "Lady of the Mammoth" heavy-bodied Earth Mother; Trickster Old Man Jackal/Fox/Coyote; the Great Bear of the Mountains; and the Dancer with Antlers.

In their quiet, conservative corner of the globe the Great Basin Indians and the nations of California were—a century ago—still living and transmitting an international body of lore—the same lore that is the foundation blocks of the "high" literatures of India, the Middle East, the Mediterranean, and Western Europe. And, just as planetary humankind becomes "ecosystem" oriented again, so the most sophisticated and agonized contemporary theologies come close to confessing that God must be a Trickster.

But God is not exactly a Trickster. Coyote the animal, Human Being the animal, Bear the animal, are just *hayakpe*—"armor" or masks—or food to be served—shapes and functions assumed in the service of the evolution of the great biosphere-being, Gaia. We slip those masks a bit to the side, and see there Coyote/Man the Trickster; Bear/Man, King of the Mountains; Deer/Mother, Queen of Compassion. In turn, those Type-Beings, Mind-created, Earth-created, are again masks. The Shining One peeks out from behind a boulder and is gone—is always there. What does Gaia, in this great space, think she's doing? But what she does is not really our concern. Our day-to-day concern is the shimmering network of gift-exchange, the ceremonies of life; energy; transformation. Our concern is the kids sleeping in the back room, snow on the far hills, a coyote howling in the sagebrush moonlight.

At this point, it is time for a reprise of Snyder's "A Berry Feast" of 1957 (reprinted in chapter 2). In that poem—which, we night say, launched Coyote on his "neopoetic" career—the Old Man is seen as the *ultimate* survivor. Snyder seems, in fact, to envision the end of civilization (1957:113):

> . . . grey dawn,
> Drenched with rain. One naked man
> Frying his horsemeat on a stone.

But Coyote survives, even though humanity may be extinct 1957:113–114):

> Coyote yaps, a knife!
> Sunrise on yellow rocks.
> People gone, death no disaster.
> Clear sun in the scrubbed sky
>   empty and bright
> Lizards scurry from darkness
> We lizards sun on yellow rocks . . .
>
> From cool springs under cedar
> On his haunches, white grin,
>
> long tongue panting, he watches:
>
> Dead city in dry summer,
> Where berries grow.

There is no shortage of references by naturalists and zoologists to the survival capacities of the coyote. Thus Leydet speaks of "all the white sheepmen and trappers who had said to me. . . . 'The coyote will be here long after we are all gone!'" 1977:77). Ryden reminds us of the coyote's adaptability:

> He can hunt either by day or by night, dine on fresh meat or survive off carrion . . . run in packs or operate as a loner. . . . The advantage to an animal of being in an unfinished state can best be demonstrated by noting the fates of those North American animals who were better perfected

for existence in their special niches [such as] the bison and the wolf. (1975:xiv)

Don Gill (1970) has shown how well coyotes have adapted to urban environments; he estimates that they are more numerous in Los Angeles now than they were in Indian times. In fact, as Nowak states,

> when the white man first arrived in North America, *Canis latrans* was distributed mainly in the western half of the continent [and in Mexico]; apparently it had disappeared from its earlier range east of Illinois. But since then it has been spreading eastward . . . in all likelihood the coyote will again occupy the entire eastern United States just as it did 10,000 years ago. (1978:12–13)

L. D. Mech adds: "The coyote has actually extended its range and filled in where the wolf was exterminated" (1978:xii–xiv).

In New England there is even evidence that the coyote has taken a new, quick step in evolution by interbreeding with the wolf and/or dog. Henry Hilton notes the possibility that the development of such "coy-wolves" may "combine the versatility of the coyote with the greater strength and aggressiveness of the wolf" (1978:210–228). As Ryden states, the hybrid animals can be seen as "filling a near-vacant predator niche" in the New England ecosphere (1975:63). Thus Native American storytellers seem to be supported by contemporary poets and biologists in seeing Coyote as the survivor par excellence, in the age of the First People as well as in our own.

In the Native American traditions, Coyote is timeless. He lived among the First People, before humans came into existence; he was often "killed," but he never died. He lives even now, skulking in meadows by day, ululating on hilltops by night; he is still often killed, but he never dies. The "mythic" Coyote and the "biological" Coyote are not two different things: they are two manifestations of a single identity. Present-day Indians, speaking either native languages or English, tell new Coyote stories, with settings either on the reservation or in the city; it's still the same Coyote. Present-day Anglo and Indian poets, writing in English, take Coyote into new worlds of the imagination; but the essence of Coyote persists.

Jarold Ramsey, scholar and poet, speaks in the voice of Coyote, reflecting on the human narrators of his story, and their listeners, and their life in the world that the First People made for them.

▼▼▼
COYOTE'S EPILOGUE TO THE TELLING

[By JAROLD RAMSEY. For Melville Jacobs and Mrs. Victoria Howard.]

And now, let us leave this story-teller
and the disjointed story he has made of us;

let us leave the fireside, the lodge of drowsy people
who inherit this world once wholly ours:
let us separate, my friends, once more, becoming
birds of the great air
fish of the endless waters
lithe animals of the forest
nimble animals of the mountains—
and I, Coyote, last to go my way,
reality's handyman, look back and grin
like a dog to think these poor listening fools,
these people who were always "coming soon,"
the story-man himself,
all will rise, and go, and burrow
deep into the winter night, full of beginnings,
their world no more perfect than before
but such as it is
enabled, empowered with our names.

In the following two excerpts from a poetry chapbook titled *Spearfish Sequence* (after a place-name in Chinook country), Dell Hymes (1981*b*) addresses Coyote from the viewpoint of twentieth-century humanity. Is it possible to hope for a "second coming" of the Transformer, of Coyote, to "make the country clean"?

▼▼▼
SPEARFISH SEQUENCE

[By DELL HYMES.]

But now it's really time—
Coyote,
Don of tricksters,

a generation is near now,
it needs to see the river
rush cold below the rimrock,

a generation is near now,
it needs the salmon,
the berries in the burnt brush—

go ahead,
finger women,
gobble food,

wander,
   finagle,
       bungle,

fall flat—
your asshole advisors will
set you straight,

so you set straight
this world before the world
this world should be.

        *   *   *

Come out—
   there you are—
Where was I?
   what happened?

Ah, you!
   if we tell,
you'll say,
   "That's just what I was thinking!"

Shall I make it "rain"
   and wash you away?

Okay, okay,
   you thought you could see Coyote,
you thought he might be coming,
   you thought he might be making the country clean;

you stared
   but it was only
a young tree wavering in the last light
   above the curve of the river.

Ah, that's just what I was thinking!
Now I've got my shit together,
   let's go.

There is, in fact, a persistent rumor among Native American people that another transformation lies ahead. Just as the First People became changed and were replaced by Humans, it is imaginable that Humans may become changed and be replaced by a totally new type of being. In a poem which envisions this possibility, David Wagoner (1978:14) does not mention Coyote specifically. However, Coyote is not only the Transformer, but also the Survivor; it is hard to conceive of a future world in which he will not find a place.

▼▼▼

SONG FOR THE FIRST PEOPLE

[From *Who Shall Be the Sun?*, by DAVID WAGONER.]

When you learned that men were coming, you changed
   into rocks,
Into fish and birds, into flowers and rivers in despair of us.
The tree under which I bend may be you,
That stone by the fire, Nighthawk swooping

And crying out over the swamp reeds, the reeds
   themselves.
Have I held you too lightly all my mornings?
I have broken your silence, dipped you up
Carelessly in my hands and drunk you, burnt you,
Carved you, slit your calm throat and danced on your skin,
Made charms of your bones. You have endured
All of it, suffering my foolishness
As the old wait quietly among clumsy children.
Now others are coming, neither like you nor like men.
I must change, First People. How do I change myself?
If no one can teach me the long will of Cedar,
Let me become Water Dog, Bitterroot, or Shut Beak.
Change me. Forgive me. I will learn to crawl, stand, or fly
Anywhere among you, forever, as though among great
   elders.

18 ▼ SUMMARY

We have met Coyote, and, as Pogo might ask—is he us? Some authors have given a positive answer, such as Ricketts: "The trickster is man, according to an archaic intuition, struggling by himself to become what he feels he must become—master of his universe." Again, the mythical trickster/transformer/culture-hero is said to be "integrated into one character, who, in reality, is none other than Man" (1965:336, 343). But if that were the whole story, then scores of Indian tribes of western North America might as well have given their mythic trickster a human name and shape, instead of that of Coyote. After all, the simultaneous manifestations of *Homo sapiens* and *Canis latrans* in Coyote can only be isolated by a kind of dangerous intellection, against which we have been warned by mythmakers, poets, and Zen masters.

As Ramsey indicates, Old Man Coyote is an especially apt "mediator" between animals and humans, between culture and nature. As such, he may be needed more than ever by modern humanity (1983:28–29). Among the American Indian tribes whose culture and language continue to flourish, the telling of Coyote stories still serves as a way of teaching traditional values—and, indeed, as a humorous way of asserting Native identity in the face of immense pressures.[1] For present-day urban Anglos, the figure of Coyote can be a reminder that Nature is still out there, after all. The following haiku by Steve Sanfield, datelined "Modesto, California," is to the point (1982:10).

Coyote calling
& suddenly it's alright
—this terrible motel.

But to say this is not to say that we have Old Man within our grasp, stabilized and taxonomized. Whether we are Indians or Anglos, writers or readers, we need to remember that, as Wendy Rose says, "Trickster turns to wind / Trickster turns to sand, / Trickster leaves you groping" (1980:71). If present-day "prostitutes, poets, Zen students and several varieties of libertine" (to quote Peter Coyote, 1982:43) attempt to arrogate the role of the Trickster to themselves, they may find themselves out-tricked, as so often happened to Old Man Coyote himself.

As Ramsey reminds us, the Trickster as mediator cannot be understood as a homogeneous figure, but only as "a dynamic interposing of the mind between polar opposites, as if affirming 'either/and . . .'" (1983:29). Whatever we say Coyote *is*, he answers, with the ancient Sanskritic sages, *Neti neti*: "That's not it, that's not it." To quote Radin:

> The symbol which Trickster embodies is not a static one. It contains within itself the promise of differentiation, the promise of god and man. For this reason every generation occupies itself with interpreting Trickster anew. No generation understands him fully, but no generation can do without him. . . . And so he became and remained everything to every man-god, animal, human being, hero, buffoon, he who was before good and evil, denier, affirmer, destroyer and creator. If we laugh at him, he grins at us. Whatever happens to him happens to us. (1972:158–159)

1: INTRODUCTION

1. Bekoff 1978 provides a data-packed volume of papers by coyote scientists, to which I will frequently refer below.

2: COYOTE IN ENGLISH LITRATURE

1. See Dobie 1949, Van Wormer 1964, Ryden 1975, and Leydet 1977. Of these works, Ryden's is especially valuable for its many firsthand observations of coyote behavior.

2. Two numbers in the last-named series are devoted entirely to Coyoteana: Bright 1978 and Kendall 1980.

An older publication which deserves special mention is Phinney 1934. Phinney was himself a Nez Perce, and he recorded an exceptionally rich collection of Coyote stories from his mother.

3. See Ramsey 1977, 1983. Also valuable is Roessel and Platero 1974. To be avoided is Lopez 1977, in which narratives "lifted" from the anthropological literature, without stated provenance, are "retold" with extreme license. There is also a whole bookshelf of Coyote stories adapted for children (e.g., Reed 1979); in these one misses not only the style of the originals, which were told for audiences of adults and children together, but also, of course, all the "best parts" of Coyote's scatological and erotic adventures.

Of some special interest is the volume *Coyote Stories*, by Mourning Dove (1934). "Mourning Dove" was the pen name of Christine Quintasket, a member of the Colville Reservation in north central Washington. Although her retelling of tribal narratives is bowdlerized, it is noteworthy as an early example of literary production among Native American women.

4. Well-known books in this mode include Rothenberg 1972 and Bran-

don 1971. Important critiques of such "reinterpretation" include Bevis 1974 and Huntsman 1983.

5. See Tedlock 1972. Linguistically responsible but esthetically effective translations of Coyote stories from northcentral California, framed in terms of "measured verse," have also recently been published by Shipley 1991.

6. My original transcriptions and translations are in Bright 1957. I have discussed problems of ethnopoetic reworking in Bright 1979 and 1982b.

7. Since 1970, an intermittent journal of new writing has been published under the name *Coyote's Journal*. A special issue in 1982 was devoted entirely to Coyoteana (Koller et al. 1982).

The poet and scholar Jarold Ramsey has also adapted Coyote for dramatic and musical performance in his theater piece *Coyote Goes Upriver* (1981) and in his cantata *The Lodge of Shadows* (Ramsey and Adler, 1976).

3: THE MYTHIC BACKGROUND

1. See Radin 1972. For another view of the trickster, see Babcock 1975.

2. Cf. Ramsey 1983:204 n. 41. Even in families of closely related languages, it is often impossible to reconstruct a common proto-form for "coyote"; e.g., in the Takic group of Southern California, Cahuilla has *ísily* (cf. the corresponding augmentative *íswet* 'wolf'), but Luiseño has *anó'*.

3. Before leaving the general topic of tricksters, I should cite the exceptionally interesting discussion of Trickster stories by Abrams and Sutton-Smith 1977. These authors' data consist primarily of Bugs Bunny cartoons and stories told by Anglo-American children of differing age groups; there is occasional comment on Native American tricksters (but no specific reference to Coyote). As a working tool, these researchers have compiled a trait list that they call a "Trickster inventory" (pp. 32–34); this should have considerable value for cross-cultural research on Trickster literature. However, it includes some features that seem relatively uncharacteristic of Coyote, and it fails to highlight such prominent Coyote traits as his wanderlust. Nevertheless, I will occasionally refer to the categories of Abrams and Sutton-Smith in my discussion below.

4: COYOTE THE WANDERER

1. Here Coyote speaks a broken version of Yurok, a neighboring Indian language.

2. Sweathouses were subterranean, and were entered by a ladder—which, in this case, Coyote had eaten.

5: COYOTE THE BRICOLEUR

1. On the northwest coast, "prairie" refers to a level grassy place surrounded by woods.

2. Ramsey (1983:9–10) points out that the bricoleur's motive for inventing death can be that of teaching human beings the meaning of compassion. We return to this point in chapter 11.

3. Cf. Kleiman and Brady (1978:175): "Some young coyotes disperse at about nine months. . . . However, coyote families under stable conditions may remain intact for much longer"—thus continuing the protected environment for learning.

6: COYOTE THE GLUTTON

1. Roasted grasshoppers, like salted peanuts, increase thirst.

7: COYOTE THE LECHER

1. Adapted from Ruth Benedict, *Tales of the Cochiti Indians*, BAE Bulletin 98 (Washington, D.C., 1931).

2. Ramsey, *Reading the Fire* (1983:44–45), gives an ethnopoetic translation of a very similar myth from the Santiam Kalapuya of Oregon.

15: COYOTE THE (HORNY) OLD MAN

1. The ancient Aztecs, too, recognized a god named Huehuecoyotl, which is quite literally "Old Man Coyote" (Kelley 1955). Although Ryden (1975:xiii) refers to the deity as a trickster, my sources identify him only as god of the dance.

16: COYOTE THE SURVIVOR

1. The poems quoted by Snyder can be found in Blue Cloud 1978 (48–51), Staple 1977 (36, 48), and MacAdams 1976 (27–28).

18: SUMMARY

1. To my misfortune, I have only heard Coyote stories as an audience of one, from narrators whose traditions survived mainly in memory. But there are tribes in which a living tradition of myth performance still continues. For accounts of such storytelling among the Navajo and Hopi, see (respectively) Toelken and Scott 1981, and Wiget 1987. The paper by Judy Trejo (1974), a Paiute woman, is an "insider's" account of the performance of Coyote stories and their significance.

REFERENCES

Abbey, Edward. 1968. *Desert Solitaire*. New York: McGraw Hill.

Abrams, David M., and Brian Sutton-Smith. 1977. The Development of the Trickster in Children's Narrative. *Journal of American Folklore* 90:29–47.

Aitken, Robert. 1982. Excerpts from *Coyote Rōshi Goroku*. In Koller et al. 1982, pp. 47–49.

Anderson, Eugene. 1965. Coyote Song. *Coyote's Journal* 4:29–35.

Andrews, Ronald D., and E. K. Boggess. 1978. Ecology of Coyotes in Iowa. In Bekoff 1978, pp. 249–265.

Aoki, Haruo. 1979. *Nez Perce Texts*. (University of California Publications in Linguistics, 90.) Berkeley: University of California Press.

Atkins, David L. 1978. Evolution and Morphology of the Coyote Brain. In Bekoff 1978, pp. 17–25.

Babcock, Barbara. 1975. "A Tolerated Margin of Mess": The Trickster and His Tales Reconsidered. *Journal of the Folklore Institute* 9:147–186. [Reprinted in *Critical Essays on Native American Literature*, ed. Andrew Wiget (Boston: G. K. Hall, 1985), pp. 153–185.]

Bekoff, Mark, ed. 1978. *Coyotes: Biology, Behavior, and Management*. New York: Academic Press.

Bennett, Bruce. 1980. *Coyote Pays a Call*. Cleveland: Bits Press, Dept. of English, Case Western Reserve University.

————. 1982. Coyote in Love. In Koller et al. 1982, p. 127.

Bevis, William. 1974. American Indian Verse Translations. *College English* 35:693–703.

Blue Cloud, Peter. 1978. *Back Then Tomorrow*. Brunswick, Me.: Blackberry Press.

————. 1982. *Elderberry Flute Song: Contemporary Coyote Tales*. Trumansburg, N.Y.: Crossing Press.

Boas, Franz. 1894. *Chinook Texts*. (Smithsonian Institution, Bureau of Ethnology, Bulletin 20.) Washington, D.C.: Government Printing Office.

————. 1901. *Kathlamet Texts*. (Smithsonian Institution, Bureau of American Ethnology, Bulletin 26.) Washington, D.C.: Government Printing Office.

Brandon, William, ed. 1971. *The Magic World: American Indian Songs and Poems*. New York: William Morrow.

Bright, William. 1954. The Travels of Coyote, a Karok Myth. *Kroeber Anthropological Society Papers* 11:1–16. [Reprinted as "Karok Coyote Stories" in *The American Indian Reader: Literature*, ed. Jeannette Henry. (San Francisco: Indian Historian Press, 1973), pp. 79–91.]

————. 1957. *The Karok Language*. (University of California Publications in Linguistics, 13.) Berkeley: University of California Press.

————. 1972. Coyote Lays Down the Law. *Language in American Indian Education*, Winter, pp. 96–98.

————. 1977. Coyote Steals Fire. *International Journal of American Linguistics, Native American Texts Series* 2:2.3–9.

————. 1979. A Karok Myth in "Measured Verse": The Translation of a Performance. *Journal of California and Great Basin Anthropology* 1:117–123. [Reprinted in Bright 1984:91–100.]

———. 1980*a*. Coyote's Journey. *American Indian Culture and Research Journal* (UCLA) 4, no. 1/2:21–48. [Reprinted in Bright 1984:101–131.]

———. 1980*b*. Coyote Gives Acorns and Salmon to Humans. In Kendall 1980, pp. 46–52.

———. 1982*a*. Poetic Structure in Oral Narrative. In *Spoken and Written Language: Exploring Orality and Literacy*, ed. Deborah Tannen, pp. 171–184. Norwood, N.J.: Ablex. [Reprinted in Bright 1984:133–148.]

———. 1982*b*. Literature: Written and Oral. *Georgetown University Round Table on Languages and Linguistics* 1981:271–283. [Reprinted in Bright 1984:79–90.]

———. 1984. *American Indian Linguistics and Literature*. Berlin: Mouton.

———. 1987. The Natural History of Old Man Coyote. In Swann and Krupat 1987, pp. 339–387.

Bright, William, ed. 1978. *Coyote Stories*. (International Journal of American Linguistics, Native American Texts Series, Monograph 1.) Chicago: University of Chicago Press.

Bright, William, and Mamie Offield. 1985. The Origin of Salmon. In *The Language of the Birds*, ed. David M. Guss, pp. 5–9. Berkeley: North Point Press.

Bright, William, and Nettie Reuben. 1982. Coyote Lays Down the Law. In Koller et al. 1982, pp. 68–71.

Buller, Galen. 1983. Comanche and Coyote, the Culture Maker. In Swann 1983, pp. 245–258.

Coyote, Peter. 1982. Muddy Prints on Mohair. In Koller et al. 1982, pp. 43–46.

Davenport, Katherine, and Lawrence Evers. n.d. *Ba'ts'oosee: An Apache Trickster Cycle*. (Transcription and translation of a videotaped performance by Rudolph Kane.) Available from Clearwater Publishing Company, New York.

de Angulo, Jaime. 1953. *Indian Tales*. New York: A. A. Wyn.

Dobie, J. Frank. 1949. *The Voice of the Coyote*. Boston: Little, Brown.

Gier, H. T., et al. 1978. Parasites and Diseases of Coyote. In Bekoff 1978, pp. 37–71.

Gill, Don. 1970. The Coyote and the Sequential Occupants of the Los Angeles Basin. *American Anthropologist* 72:821–826.

Gill, Don, and Penelope Bonnett. 1973. Los Angeles: A City with Islands of Wild Landscape. In *Nature in the Urban Landscape*, pp. 87–108. Baltimore: York Press.

Hill, Jane H., and Rosinda Nolasquez. 1973. *Mulu'wetam: The First People. Cupeño Oral History and Language*. Banning, Ca.: Malki Museum Press.

Hilton, Henry. 1978. Systematics and Ecology of the Eastern Coyote. In Bekoff 1978, pp. 210–228.

Hinton, Leanne. 1978. Coyote Baptizes the Chickens. In Bright 1978, pp. 117–120.

Huntsman, Jeffrey F. 1983. Traditional Native American Literature: The Translation Dilemma. In Swann 1983, pp. 87–97.

Hymes, Dell. 1978. *Fivefold Fanfare for Coyote*. Portland, Or.: Corvine Press.

———. 1981a. *"In Vain I Tried to Tell You": Essays in Native American Ethnopoetics*. Philadelphia: University of Pennsylvania Press.

————. 1981b. *Spearfish Sequence*. Cambridge, Ma.: Corvine Press.

Jung, Carl. 1972. On the Psychology of the Trickster Figure. In Radin 1972, pp. 195–211.

Kelley, David H. 1955. Quetzalcoatl and His Coyote Origins. *El México Antiguo* 8:397–416.

Kendall, Martha B., ed. 1980. *Coyote Stories II*. (International Journal of American Linguistics, Native American Texts Series, Monograph 6.) Chicago: University of Chicago Press.

Kennelly, James J. 1978. Coyote Reproduction. In Bekoff 1978, pp. 73–93.

Kleiman, D. G., and C. A. Brady. 1978. Coyote Behavior in the Context of Recent Canid Research. In Bekoff 1978, pp. 163–188.

Koller, James, et al., eds. 1982. *Coyote's Journal*. Berkeley: Wingbow.

Kroeber, A. L. 1972. *More Mohave Myths*. (Anthropological Records, 27.) Berkeley: University of California Press.

Laird, Carobeth. 1984. *Mirror and Pattern: George Laird's World of Chemehuevi Mythology*. Banning, Ca.: Malki Museum Press.

Lamadrid, Enrique R. 1972. *Cantos del Coyote*. Albuquerque: Associated Gold Street Olive Press.

Lehner, Philip N. 1978. Coyote Communication. In Bekoff 1978, pp. 128–162.

Leydet, François. 1977. *The Coyote: Defiant Songdog of the West*. San Francisco: Chronicle Books.

Lopez, Barry Holstun. 1977. *Giving Birth to Thunder, Sleeping with His Daughter: Coyote Builds North America*. Kansas City: Sheed Andrews & McMeel.

MacAdams, Lewis. 1976. *News from Niman Farm*. Bolinas, Ca.: Tombouctou.

Mattina, Anthony. 1987. North American Indian Mythography: Editing Texts for the Printed Page. In Swann and Krupat 1987, pp. 129–148.

Mech, L. David. 1978. Foreword. In Bekoff 1978, pp. xii–xiv.

Minta, Kathryn A., and Steven C. Minta. 1991. Partners in Carnivory: North America's Coyotes and Badgers Have an Ancient Bond. *Natural History*, June, pp. 60–63.

Mourning Dove (Christine Quintasket). 1934. *Coyote Stories*. Caldwell, Idaho: Caxton Printers. [Reprinted, Lincoln: University of Nebraska Press, 1990.]

Murie, Adolph. 1940. *Ecology of the Coyote in the Yellowstone*. (U.S. Dept. of the Interior, National Park Service, Fauna Series, 4.) Washington, D.C.: Government Printing Office.

Nowak, Ronald M. 1978. Evolution and Taxonomy of Coyotes and Related Canids. In Bekoff 1978, pp. 3–16.

Ortiz, Simon. 1977. *A Good Journey*. Berkeley: Turtle Island.

Phinney, Archie. 1934. *Nez Percé Texts*. (Columbia University Contributions to Anthropology, 25.) New York: Columbia University.

Pringle, Laurence. 1977. *The Controversial Coyote: Predation, Politics, and Ecology*. New York: Harcourt Brace.

Radin, Paul. 1972. *The Trickster: A Study in American Indian Mythology*, 2d ed. New York: Shocken.

Ramsey, Jarold. 1973. *Love in an Earthquake*. Seattle: University of Washington Press.

———. 1977. *Coyote Was Going There: Indian Literature of the Oregon Country*. Seattle: University of Washington Press.

———. 1981. Coyote Goes Upriver: A Cycle for Story-Theater and Mime. *Georgia Review* 35:524–551.

———. 1983. *Reading the Fire: Essays in the Traditional Indian Literatures of the Far West*. Lincoln: University of Nebraska Press.

———. n.d. Coyote's Epilogue to the Telling. Unpublished ms.

Ramsey, Jarold, and Samuel Adler. 1976. *The Lodge of Shadows: A Cantata*. New York: Carl Fischer.

Reed, Evelyn Dahl. 1979. *The Misadventures of Coyote*. New York: Vantage Press.

Ricketts, Mac Linscott. 1965. The North American Indian Trickster. *History of Religions* 5:327–350.

Roessel, Robert A., Jr., and Dillon Platero, eds. 1974. *Coyote Stories of the Navajo People*, 2d ed. Phoenix: Navajo Curriculum Center Press.

Rose, Wendy. 1980. *Lost Copper*. Banning, Ca.: Malki Museum Press.

Rothenberg, Jerome, ed. 1972. *Shaking the Pumpkin: Traditional Poetry of the Indian North Americas*. Garden City: Doubleday.

Ryden, Hope. 1975. *God's Dog*. Harmondsworth and New York: Penguin.

Sanfield, Steve. 1982. A Few for Coyote. In Koller et al. 1982, pp. 10–11.

Sapir, Edward. 1910. *Yana Texts*. (University of California Publications in American Archaeology and Ethnology, 9:1.) Berkeley: University of California Press.

———. 1930. *Southern Paiute*. 3 vols. (Proceedings of the

American Academy of Arts and Sciences, 65.) Boston: American Academy of Arts and Sciences.

Shipley, William. 1991. *The Maidu Indian Myths and Stories of Hanc'ibyjim*. Berkeley: Heyday Press.

Silko, Leslie. 1981. *Storyteller*. New York: Seaver.

Snyder, Gary. 1957. A Berry Feast. *Evergreen Review* 2:110–114. [Reprinted in *The Back Country*, pp. 13–16. New York: New Directions, 1968.]

———. 1977. *The Old Ways*. San Francisco: City Lights.

Staple, Will. 1977. *Passes for Human*. Berkeley: Shaman Drum.

Swann, Brian, ed. 1983. *Smoothing the Ground: Essays in Native American Oral Literature*. Berkeley and Los Angeles: University of California Press.

Swann, Brian, and Arnold Krupat, eds. 1987. *Recovering the Word: Essays on Native American Literature*. Berkeley: University of California Press.

Tedlock, Dennis. 1972. *Finding the Center: Narrative Poetry of the Zuni Indians*. New York: Dial.

Toelken, Barre. 1971. Ma'i Joldloshi: Legendary Styles and Navajo Myth. In *American Folk Legend*, ed. Wayland Hand, pp. 203–211. Berkeley: University of California Press.

———. 1976. The "Pretty Languages" of Yellowman: Genre, Mode, and Texture in Navajo Coyote Narratives. In *Folklore Genres*, ed. Dan Ben-Amos, pp. 145–170. Austin: University of Texas Press.

Toelken, Barre, and Tacheeni Scott. 1981. Poetic Retranslation and the "Pretty Languages" of Yellowman. *Traditional American Indian Literatures*, ed. Karl Kroeber, pp. 65–116. Lincoln: University of Nebraska Press.

Trejo, Judy. 1974. Coyote Tales: A Paiute Commentary. *Journal of American Folklore* 87:66–81.

Twain, Mark. 1913. *Roughing It.* New York: Harper.

Tyler, Hamilton. 1975. *Pueblo Animals and Myths.* Norman: University of Oklahoma Press.

Van Wormer, Joe. 1964. *The World of the Coyote.* Philadelphia: Lippincott.

Wagoner, David. 1978. *Who Shall Be the Sun?* Bloomington: Indiana University Press.

Wiget, Andrew. 1987. Telling the Tale: A Performance Analysis of a Hopi Coyote Story. In Swann and Krupat 1987, pp. 255–296.

Young, Stanley Paul, and H. H. T. Jackson. 1951. *The Clever Coyote.* Harrisburg: Stackpole.

INDEX

Designer:	Seventeenth Street Studios
Compositor:	Wilsted & Taylor
Text:	10.5/14 New Baskerville
Display:	Copperplate and New Baskerville
Printer:	Edwards Brothers, Inc.
Binder:	Edwards Brothers, Inc.